MONDAYS
with JESUS
2016

RENEE ANDREWS

Cover art and design by Gina Brown Art
www.GinaBrownArt.com

Interior format by The Killion Group
http://thekilliongroupinc.com

DEDICATIONS

For our children:
Rene and Ariel Zeringue
Kaleb and Kaiyla Zeringue
Matt and Brittany McCallum

And our grandchildren:
Alanus, Jerry and Naomi Zeringue
Ryan and Brooks McCallum
and all the grandchildren yet to come

OTHER BOOKS AVAILABLE

Devotional
Mondays with Jesus 2015

Christian Fiction
Profiled
Her Valentine Family
Healing Autumn's Heart
Picture Perfect Family
Love Reunited
Heart of a Rancher
Bride Wanted
Yuletide Twins
Mommy Wanted
Small-Town Billionaire
Daddy Wanted
Family Wanted
Baby Wanted

MONDAY, JANUARY 4

"For you were once darkness, but now you are light in the Lord. Live as children of light." ~ Ephesians 5:8

Recently, some pranksters decided to have fun at the Denver airport and put stickers that looked like power outlets on the walls. They then videoed travelers, cell phones and computers in hand, attempting to "plug in" to the fictitious outlets.

If you've been to any airport, this isn't difficult to visualize. In fact, if you've been to any modern, crowded location, you've undoubtedly seen clusters of people sitting as close as possible to the nearest power supply. People need that power; they are drawn to it for their communication needs.

Likewise, when we need to recharge our souls, we search for an appropriate source to supply that need. Do you have a "go to" person when you're feeling down? Who do you call? Who do you visit? Does someone see you as that "go to" person? Can they count on you to lift them up?

Christ called us the light of the world. As His children, we are to be a source of spiritual energy to those around us.

Undoubtedly, throughout this new year, you will interact with individuals who are experiencing a spiritual low. Perhaps they are feeling guilty for a past sin. Or they're going through a difficult time financially. Health issues may be challenging. Friendships have disintegrated. Family units have been broken. They are looking for a source of power, a light in a dark world.

This year, immerse yourself in the Word. Fill your thoughts with Christ. When others come to you to recharge their souls, let them find that you have exactly what they need, the love of Christ.

This Week: When you plug in your phone, computer, visualize plugging in spiritually as well. Then open your Bible and read, bow your head and pray...and recharge. And if you know of a friend or family member going through a spiritual low, call them today. Don't wait for them to contact you. Let them know that you love them and are praying for them. Let them know that if they need you, you are available. Don't let them find that you're merely pretending, like those fake stickers on the wall. Give them what they need. Be the light in the world!

My Prayer to Start this Week:

Those to Remember in Prayer this Week:

MONDAY, JANUARY 11

"Come and hear, all you who fear God; let me tell you what he has done for me." ~ Psalm 66:16

I remember the cars my Granny Bowers drove throughout the years of my youth. One was a white Buick LeSabre, which was followed by a gold Buick LeSabre (obviously, my grandparents liked the model, because when she had her gold one, my Paw Paw Bowers had one too, also gold). But it was always easy to tell their cars apart, because Granny's car had the same tag that had graced each and every one of her vehicles for as long as I could remember. A beat up white tag with plain black letters. Nothing fancy, but the words definitely got the point across:

LET ME TELL YOU ABOUT MY GRANDCHILDREN.

I have to admit that, in spite of the fact that there were a dozen grandkids in the Bowers family, I felt special each and every time I saw that tag, whether in the driveway at their house or in the parking lot of the church or driving down the street of our neighborhood (we lived a mile away from my grandparents). But the reason I felt special wasn't because the tag referred to me; it was because I knew she meant every word. Granny, like many grandparents, was always ready, willing and able to tell everyone about her precious grandchildren.

I know how that feels, the desire to boast and brag, since I now have grandchildren of my own. And I do love to talk about them, because I love them. I am proud of them. But there is someone even more prominent than those precious children that I should also be as eager to talk about, to brag about. And I visualize another tag, one that should be written on my heart, mind and soul:

LET ME TELL YOU ABOUT MY LORD.

It's so easy to talk about our children or grandchildren, to find sheer joy in even the smallest things that they've done or said or planned. Shouldn't it be that easy to talk about Christ? About the colossal things that He's done—like dying for our sins. And said—that He will come again. And planned—a place for us to spend eternity with Him.

This Week: When you find yourself bragging about your children, grandchildren, spouse or friend, take the opportunity to also brag about the One who gives eternal life. Visualize a white tag, black letters, stating: LET ME TELL YOU ABOUT MY LORD.

My Prayer to Start this Week:

Those to Remember in Prayer this Week:

MONDAY, JANUARY 18

"Have nothing to do with the fruitless deeds of darkness, but rather expose them." ~ Ephesians 5:11

Writers discussing plots will often shake their heads when a protagonist does something irrational that will most certainly cause imminent harm. We classify the character as "T.S.T.L.," or too-stupid-to-live. I know it sounds cruel, but picture this (it won't be hard, since you've certainly read a similar scene in a novel or witnessed it in a movie):

A group of teens are gathered in a remote location, such as a cabin in the woods. Recently, several people have gone missing in those woods, hence the temptation to prove they can stay an entire night. They hear a noise outside. One of the group says he or she will check it out. This person walks outside potentially—and most likely—heading directly toward danger. Perhaps they do it out of a desire to be brave, or maybe because they are intrigued by the darkness. But the end result is always the same. They are as lost as those previous victims, falling prey to whatever evildoer waits in the dark shadows. Every writer hearing this portion of the plot would say the same thing: "T.S.T.L."

The concept of T.S.T.L. can also be applied to our spiritual lives. Why do we leave the nice, warm cabin to head into, or even return to, the cold, lonely darkness of sin? We all have that temptation hovering in the distance, something that tries to lure you from your Lord and awaits to suck you in, pull you away from the light, never to be seen again.

That is the devil's desire.

How can we combat his efforts? Surround yourself in the light. Immerse yourself in the power of the Holy Spirit. What would have happened if the remainder of the group would have said—or better yet, screamed—DON'T GO!

Have you surrounded yourselves with friends that will help you stay in the light? Or have you ventured toward those who are pushing you into the darkness, maybe even leading the way? I have a "life group" that I meet with each week for an informal Bible study. We discuss more than the Bible; we discuss our lives, our temptations, and how we are striving to stay in the light. Away from the darkness. And I know that if any of them saw me straying toward the edge of the woods, I'd definitely hear those words: DON'T GO! And I would listen, because I'd have no doubt that they were keeping me out of the T.S.T.L status. Because they want me to live, not only on earth, but also for eternity.

This Week: Take inventory of your friends and of the current distance between you and the darkness of temptation. Decide whether you have the kind of support group you need to help you steer clear of the T.S.T.L status. Move toward the light. Immerse yourself in it and surround yourself with those who will be there for you, as you are there for them, working together toward that end goal—eternity with our Lord.

My Prayer to Start this Week:

Those to Remember in Prayer this Week:

MONDAY, JANUARY 25

"When someone invites you to a wedding feast, do not take the place of honor, for a person more distinguished than you may have been invited. If so, the host who invited both of you will come and say to you, 'Give this person your seat.' Then, humiliated, you will have to take the least important place. But when you are invited, take the lowest place, so that when your host comes, he will say to you, 'Friend, move up to a better place.' Then you will be honored in the presence of all the other guests." Luke 14:8-10

Lessons in humility are often served with a jab to the gut, aren't they? But it doesn't hurt to be brought down to earth a bit (or a lot) when we find ourselves feeling a bit haughty.

At my very first book signing, I received a man-sized dose of humility. I was absolutely thrilled to be asked to sign at a large bookstore in Tampa with several other, much more notable authors. When the signing ended, I proceeded to the checkout area to purchase several books written by my writer friends. As the young man at the register scanned the books, I exclaimed, "I just had my first book signing. I wrote a book!"

Rather than looking impressed, he waved a hand toward the stacks and said, "Lots of people do."

And I knew that he was right. This was a major book chain, with books filling every nook and cranny. Mine barely made a dent in the surface. But I admit that I was feeling a bit prideful that day, and he put me back in my place. Yes, I'd accomplished a goal on earth, but it doesn't come near to the only goal that matters: living with Christ, on earth and for eternity.

This Week: When you're tempted to boast about something you deem big in your world, remember that Christ's example of washing the disciples' feet is the way He lived, the way He served...and He was flawless. Perfect. Had every reason to brag and boast. Yet he washed their feet. Swallow that urge to brag. Nurture that desire to serve without being seen. If you're meant to sit at the head of the table or be the center of attention, let someone else put you there. Experience the beauty of humility. Obviously, I'm still learning, but I do have people—like that sales clerk—who remind me when I forget ;)

My Prayer to Start This Week:

Those to Remember in Prayer this Week:

MONDAY, FEBRUARY 1

"And will not God bring about justice for his chosen ones, who cry out to him day and night? Will he keep putting them off?" ~ *Luke 18:7*

In the verse above, Christ is telling his disciples the parable about the persistent widow and the unfair judge. The widow continues to ask the judge for justice against her enemies. Over and over she asks, and over and over, he ignores her request. Until finally, he grows weary of her repetition, and he grants her desire.

The story reminds me of a quote from social reformer Jacob Riis: "Look at a stone cutter hammering away at his rock, perhaps a hundred times without as much as a crack showing in it. Yet at the hundred-and-first blow it will split in two, and I know it was not the last blow that did it, but all that had gone before."

The quote from Jacob Riis, which is so descriptive and inspirational that the San Antonio Spurs have it painted in their locker room, is a rendition of Jesus' parable about the widow. The widow could have given up the first time the judge said no. She could have given up the second. But she didn't, and eventually, he said yes. Likewise, the stone cutter could have stopped hitting the rock after the fiftieth blow, or after the ninetieth, but he didn't, and on that hundred-and-first blow, the stone cracked.

I've been guilty of praying for a season, or praying until I believe God should've answered my request, and then giving up. What if I stopped just before the judge would have said yes? Or what if I quit after the ninety-ninth blow? God, like that judge and like that stone cutter, knows the value of persistence. He appreciates us believing enough in His mighty power to hear us when we continue to ask. He sees our faith. And if He deems our request should be granted, or perhaps our persistence causes Him to change His mind (since He does as He pleases – Psalm 115:3 and Daniel 4:35), then why should we stop asking?

This Week: Do you have a prayer that you can't see God answering? Continue to pray. Do you have a friend that you've tried to bring to Christ, and yet they remain uninterested? Continue to show them Christ through you. Be the persistent widow. Be the stone cutter. Go for the hundred-and-first blow. PUSH—Pray Until Something Happens.

My Prayer to Start this Week:

Those to Remember in Prayer this Week:

MONDAY, FEBRUARY 8

"If anyone, then, knows the good they ought to do and doesn't do it, it is sin for them." James 4:17

While J.R. and I were sharing a meal with friends, we discussed a job that an acquaintance had taken. The position paid well, but put the person in an undeniably tempting situation toward sin. My friend's husband asked, "Is it really worth risking her soul?"

This reminded me of other situations where job opportunities caused friends to potentially go astray. When I was in middle school, video recorders and players (Video Cassette Recorders, or VCRs) were the "big thing." That was the Christmas gift everyone wanted, followed by a bunch of videos to play on your VCR.

The next "big thing" with regard to that industry was the video rental store. One of the deacons at our church quickly realized the potential for making money by owning a video rental store. He opened the first rental store in our town and did well quickly. But then he was questioned about the R-rated movies that he made available in the store. *"How can you call yourself a Christian and condone those type of movies, even making them easily accessible to the community?"*

A more recent job situation happened with a Christian gentleman who took a position at a large used car dealership in town. Upon starting the position, he was trained on how to deceive customers. Seriously. They schooled him on how to steer them toward a purchase that might not be in their best interest; they taught him how to get them to make a purchase, even if it might cripple them financially. The place had a checklist of things to say and do, based on what the customer said or did. Basically, whatever it took to get them to buy the car (and pay too much for it) was not only requested but demanded to be considered a successful salesman.

What happened to both of these men? The first one, when confronted about the questionable movies, sold his portion of the business to his business partner. The second one quit his used car salesman position after just four days. He said he couldn't sleep at night knowing he was getting paid to deceive.

Now, I'm not saying that every used car salesman deceives his customers. In fact, I know of one who is honest and discloses everything about the vehicles he sells. But I do think that with any occupation that allows more success based on lax morals, a Christian must answer the same question our friend asked: "Is it worth risking your soul?"

This Week: If your current environment, be it work or school or play, isn't spiritually healthy, consider doing what the video store owner and used car salesman did. Make a change. Pray for God's help and remove yourself from the temptation. Don't risk your soul.

My Prayer to Start this Week:

Those to Remember in Prayer this Week:

MONDAY, FEBRUARY 15

"For he chose us in him before the creation of the world to be holy and blameless in his sight." ~ Ephesians 1:4

A few weeks ago, J.R. and I had the opportunity to hear our son Kaleb speak to his youth group in Montgomery. The title of his lesson was "Labels." I have to tell you that I would have loved for someone to have given me the same information when I was a teen. But even for adults, labels can control our lives, not only the labels we are given by others, but the ones we give ourselves.

It isn't difficult to see what labels people bestow on themselves if you are around them for any length of time. Kaleb gave some examples of the negative labels that teens often identify with: forgetful, clumsy, nerdy, class clown, failure, ugly, shy, ashamed.

Our past experiences coupled with what we have been told by those in authority create our personal labels. But the labels we give ourselves or that are given to us by others are not the ones that count. The only labels that really count are the ones given to us when we were created—the ones given to us by God.

God's labels for us: child of God, friend of Jesus, accepted, new, righteous, son in Christ, daughter in Christ, heir to His kingdom, blessed, forgiven.

And the label that comes from the verse I quoted above: chosen.

This Week: Ignore the labels given to you by society and focus on the labels blessed upon you by God. Remember that, with Christ, you are chosen, and you are new!

"Therefore, if anyone is in Christ, the new creation has come: The old has gone, the new is here!" 2 Corinthians 5:17

My Prayer to Start this Week:

Those to Remember in Prayer this Week:

MONDAY, FEBRUARY 22

"Therefore I tell you, whatever you ask for in prayer, believe that you have received it, and it will be yours." ~ Mark 11:24

Alanus and Jerry, our oldest grandsons, spent the night with us last night. As usual, they each said their prayer before bed, but this time I noticed something I hadn't noticed before in the way that they pray. Here is a portion of the prayer that each of them recited last night:

"Dear God, Thank you for letting us have a good day at school, and thank you for letting us do good and score goals at soccer. Thank you for letting us spend the night at Pops' and KK's house. Thank you for letting us go to Waffle House in the morning for breakfast. Thank you for letting us get a Kit Kat for our snack tomorrow. Thank you for letting us have a good day at school tomorrow."

They've prayed this way for as long as I can remember, but I never paid attention to what they are actually doing. Both boys pray for the following day's events as though God has already granted their request. Did they know that we would take them to Waffle House for breakfast? We hadn't mentioned it, but after hearing the prayer, naturally, we leaned that direction (we're grandparents, after all). Did they know that I had bought them a Kit Kat for snack? They suspected, but they didn't know for sure. Did they know that they would have a good day at school today? No, but they thanked God for the good day in advance.

Alanus and Jerry pray as if they have already received their request from the Lord. I tried to recall if I have ever prayed that way. Yes, I try. I may pray for God to allow us to have a great day or accomplish a difficult goal that we have on our upcoming agenda. I've even prayed a few times that my children's sports teams would win during a close game (okay, a lot of times). But I can't say that I ever totally convinced myself that God was going to do what I requested simply because I asked.

Maybe the reason is that I feel I'm asking for something I don't deserve. Or maybe it's because I figure God knows that the answer I need isn't the one I want (sounds like I'm trying to second guess Him, doesn't it?).

I wonder what would happen if I went all-in when I pray. Thank God for the things that haven't even come about, for the healing that the doctors say isn't possible, for the financial relief that appears out of the picture, for the mending of a relationship that seems beyond hope?

God, give me the courage to pray like Alanus and Jerry. Grant me the faith to start thanking you in advance! Faith of a child–it's an amazing thing, isn't it?

This Week: Alter the direction of your prayers this week. Pray like my grandsons. Thank God in advance!

My Prayer to Start this Week:

Those to Remember in Prayer this Week:

MONDAY, FEBRUARY 29

"Do not judge, or you too will be judged. For in the same way you judge others, you will be judged, and with the measure you use, it will be measured to you. Why do you look at the speck of sawdust in your brother's eye and pay no attention to the plank in your own eye? How can you say to your brother, 'Let me take the speck out of your eye,' when all the time there is a plank in your own eye? You hypocrite, first take the plank out of your own eye, and then you will see clearly to remove the speck from your brother's eye." Matthew 7:1-5

My husband is a former All-American gymnast and owns a tumbling gym near our home. The location is great, plenty of traffic and easily accessible from several sections of town. Until last week, we had never had any theft occur at the business. But last Wednesday, at 6:30 in the evening (still daylight), a woman's purse was stolen out of her car. She'd just bought the vehicle two weeks before, and the guy who took the purse not only busted the glass but warped the frame around the window while breaking into the car.

When the police officer arrived, he asked if anyone saw anything suspicious. Several of our clients had noticed a large gray truck parked beside the woman's car. None had seen the truck at our business before. I had also noticed the truck and jumped on the bandwagon describing it to the officer, while several people who saw the large man inside the truck did their best to describe him as well. It was easily deduced from the tone of description about this man we'd never seen before that everyone believed the "guy in the gray truck" had parked in our lot with the intention of stealing and taken the purse after seeing the woman enter the gym.

Naturally, the officer wrote down all of the information and kindly reminded everyone that they could not press charges against the "guy in the gray truck" without evidence. We were dismayed that the man had gotten away with the robbery.

Fast-forward to the next day, when my husband remembered that the business across the street had a surveillance camera pointed at the exact area of our parking lot where the break-in occurred. He asked to review the video footage, and after two hours of watching the tapes, he watched the man in the gray truck leave our parking lot. A while later, a small red sports car rushed into the parking lot, took the space beside the woman's car, got out, bashed her window, took her purse and left...in the span of sixty seconds.

The man in the gray truck ended up being the parent of a child who takes classes at the gym. The people who described the guy in the gray truck (including me) were served a nice dose of bitter stop-judging medicine.

The police are still looking for the man in the red sports car. And I am still trying to come to terms with how easily I judged and silently condemned a man who was completely innocent.

Though this case was a more obvious and outspoken form of judging, I know that I am also guilty of subtle judgment, forming a conclusion about someone or something without waiting until the facts have played out, without taking time to view the video footage. Christ didn't mince words when he told us not to judge others. If I am truly going to follow Him, then I need to remember that when I point one finger at someone else...the rest of my fingers are pointing back to me.

This Week: At some point in your life, you formed a misconception about someone that, once you realized the error of your opinion, became a dear friend. Say a prayer of thanks to God for putting that person in your life and for letting you see through the fog of your judgmental nature.

My Prayer to Start this Week:

Those to Remember in Prayer this Week:

MONDAY, MARCH 7

"Now when Daniel learned that the decree had been published, he went home to his upstairs room where the windows opened toward Jerusalem. Three times a day he got down on his knees and prayed, giving thanks to his God, just as he had done before." Daniel 6:10

A couple of weeks ago, a group from our church went to see War Room. War Room is one of the most powerful, inspirational movies I've ever seen. I won't spoil it for you, but even from the preview you learn that the "war room" depicted in the movie is actually a closet in an elderly woman's home. She refers to it as her "war room," because that is where she plans her battle strategy against the devil. Her prayers are documented, with the dates that she made her requests to God as well as the dates those requests were answered. It's a beautiful, power concept, and I left with a renewed determination to spend more time in prayer with God.

Though the movie is new, the idea isn't. In fact, we read about war rooms in the Bible. In the verse above, Daniel goes to his upstairs room, "just as he had done before," which tells us that this is a usual practice.

Though the war room was an actual room in the movie and also with Daniel, our war room doesn't have to consist of four walls. In Luke 5:16, we learn that Jesus often withdrew to lonely places to pray. He removed himself from distractions and concentrated on talking to His Father. When J.R. and I take long trips on the Goldwing, my personal war room becomes the backseat of a motorcycle. I find it very easy to have a conversation with my Maker about the beautiful world He created when I'm observing it so clearly.

Regardless of where your war room happens to be, it is important to have a place where you know you can plead your case to God. Tell him about your struggles. Pray for yourself. Pray for others. Pray for financial struggles. Pray for emotional struggles. Pray for physical struggles. Pray to praise Him for everything wonderful in your life. Pray to praise Him for the eternal life to come. Make an appointment each day that trumps everything else on your to-do list...a time to head to your war room and plan your strategy with your Lord.

This Week: See the War Room movie. If you've seen it before, watch it again. Remind yourself of the importance to spend time with your Lord on a usual basis. Make your own war room, and like Miss Clara in the movie, let that room become your most used, favorite room in the house!

My Prayer to Start this Week:

Those to Remember in Prayer this Week:

MONDAY, MARCH 14

"Who is going to harm you if you are eager to do good? But even if you should suffer for what is right, you are blessed. Do not fear their threats; do not be frightened. But in your hearts revere Christ as Lord. Always be prepared to give an answer to everyone who asks you to give the reason for the hope that you have. But do this with gentleness and respect, keeping a clear conscience, so that those who speak maliciously against your good behavior in Christ may be ashamed of their slander. For it is better, if it is God's will, to suffer for doing good than for doing evil." 1 Peter 3:13-17

Yesterday, our two oldest grandsons came to our house after school because their parents had gone to the hospital in Birmingham to visit friends who had a baby. Alanus and Jerry had a soccer practice scheduled for 5:30, but the skies were dark, and we didn't think the practice would be held. However, at 5:00, the coach hadn't sent a text canceling, so the boys got dressed and we headed to the community college for practice.

Sure enough, as we pulled into the parking area, the dark clouds opened, and rain doused everything in sight. Another grandmother had arrived earlier than I did, and she and her grandson were already out on the field when the rain started. While my grandboys and I watched, she and the boy started running off the field, but then the little boy said something, and the grandmother stopped. And laughed. Then the two of them ran in the rain, not toward the car, but around the field. It wasn't lightning, and we didn't hear thunder; it was simply very wet. And they had an absolute blast playing in the rain.

I loved the way this lady handled what could have been a dismal afternoon with her grandson. In my opinion, it was a beautiful example of making lemonade out of lemons. I assume this woman probably tackles all of life's events the same way.

Life deals us lemons at times, doesn't it? We may be going through difficult health issues, having relationship troubles, suffering through financial distress. Problems of the world can rain on us in the same manner that the downpour soaked that grandmother and her grandson yesterday. And we can let ourselves drown. Or we can stop, see that the storm is only temporary, because one way or another, the storm will pass...even if that doesn't happen until we begin eternity with our Lord.

Whether on this earth or after, we are promised that sweet lemonade.

This Week: The next time you have the opportunity, take a moment to enjoy the rain and thank God that He always provides lemonade for those "lemon" days.

My Prayer to Start this Week:

Those to Remember in Prayer this Week:

MONDAY, MARCH 21

"On the evening of that first day of the week, when the disciples were together, with the doors locked for fear of the Jewish leaders, Jesus came and stood among them and said, "Peace be with you!" After he said this, he showed them his hands and side. The disciples were overjoyed when they saw the Lord." ~ John 20:19-20

Have you ever wondered what the disciples were doing on that achingly long Saturday between the crucifixion and the resurrection? Based on the verses above, the disciples were hiding, with the doors locked for fear of the Jewish leaders, on that first Easter Sunday.

There have been times in my life, particularly through some of my high school years and then on into the first of my college years, that I couldn't feel God. I didn't see him as clearly as I have at any other time in my life. My spiritual life was at its weakest, and I honestly didn't know if I was anything that God wanted. I took an excessive load of classes in college, because I couldn't wait to get out and get a "real job." I also worked third shift as a computer operator, because I couldn't wait to have money in my bank account and prove I had made it, that I was successful, and that I could be the independent person I'd dreamed of being.

But in that pursuit of the American dream, I forgot the One who made all dreams possible. Maybe "forgot" is too strong a term, but I definitely didn't have God at the front of my list of my priorities. He wasn't even a close second.

Nevertheless, I know now, when I think back to the times I felt most alone, He was still there, knocking, waiting, reminding me in subtle ways…He still wanted me. I simply had to turn back to Him.

Thank God I found my way home.

I think about that dark time of my life, and I acquaint it to that quiet Saturday, when the disciples couldn't see their Lord, when they couldn't feel Him the way they'd felt him for the three preceding years. They were frightened. Afraid. Locking themselves behind closed doors.

But when they saw Him again, they experienced joy, the same joy that I experienced when I finally looked…and saw my Lord again.

This Week: If you've turned your back on Christ, lost your way and aren't sure whether He would even want you anymore, remember what those disciples learned on that lengthy Saturday and what I learned throughout those trying years: the silence of God doesn't mean the absence of God. He is waiting, and He wants you back!

My Prayer to Start this Week:

Those to Remember in Prayer this Week:

MONDAY, MARCH 28

"He asked her, 'Woman, why are you crying? Who is it you are looking for?' Thinking he was the gardener, she said, 'Sir, if you have carried him away, tell me where you have put him, and I will get him.' Jesus said to her, 'Mary.' She turned toward him and cried out in Aramaic, 'Rabboni!' (which means "Teacher")." ~ John 20:15-16

I've often been thrown by Mary Magdalene's assumption when she first saw Jesus after the resurrection. She thought he was the gardener? The Lord and Savior that she'd been mourning? Worshipping? Spending countless time with prior to his crucifixion? Yet she thought he was the gardener. Understatement of the century.

Granted, I do not understand the manner in which Christ's appearance was different after he rose from the grave; however, I do know that after He spoke her name, she recognized her Lord.

I've mourned loved ones who have passed on, and I understand the way grief confuses your senses. You become numb to the world around you, where you might not even see what is directly in front of you, even if, in Mary Magdalene's case, it's the very One she mourned.

Have you ever fallen prey to being so absorbed in your own world, or in the circumstances currently taking control of your life, that you can no longer see the Savior? We try so hard to fix things ourselves, to worry about something as though our apprehension will actually make a difference in the outcome, instead of looking to the One who is right there, waiting to help, and guaranteeing that we see the Light at the end of our dark tunnel. Because He is the light!

This Week: Have you been so lost in your own world that, like Mary, you can't see the One waiting to show you the way through every storm, trouble and trial of life? Remember the One who rose to set you free, and let Him have His way. He will carry you through the darkness, bear your burden and guide you safely through the storm so that you can be with Him in the light that will span eternity.

My Prayer to Start this Week:

Those to Remember in Prayer this Week:

MONDAY, APRIL 4

"Carry each other's burdens, and in this way you will fulfill the law of Christ." ~ Galatians 6:2

Last night at our life group Bible study, we discussed what Christians actually "do" for other Christians. The discussion centered around encouragement, edification, building one another up. Plenty of heads bobbed in agreement. In fact, I'd say the tone for the class was extremely *comfortable*.

Then a dear friend spoke up and said that it was difficult to admit, but that she'd been having a hard time recently. She went on to share that when she walked through the church building yesterday morning, lots of people asked how she was doing, and she answered all with, "I'm fine." And she said everyone she asked had the same response. Everyone smiled. Everyone seemed happy. Everyone claimed they were fine. But then, when she exited the church, she realized she wasn't fine and hadn't been "fine" in weeks. And as she examined her own emotions, she wondered if all of those people smiling and saying they were fine…actually weren't fine at all.

With her confession, the flood gates opened for our group. Everyone started sharing their low points, some that had happened recently and others that had passed without the group ever knowing about the difficulty. It seems we didn't share because a) we didn't want to burden our brothers and sisters in Christ, or b) we have a hard time admitting we don't have it all together.

That life group meeting was one of the most emotional, most powerful Bible studies I've ever experienced. Why? Because we went beyond the surface. We didn't merely say what we thought everyone wanted to hear. We bore each other's burdens together, just as we are commanded to do in Galatians 6:2.

The result was incredible. I woke this morning feeling as though I don't have to bear problems alone. I don't have to worry or feel I have no one to talk to when things are tough. Yes, I can and will pray for help and guidance when I'm having a difficult time, but I also have a bounty of Christian friends waiting to help me, to lift my spirits when I'm down. And next time, when they ask me how I'm doing, I won't merely give the patent answer. If I am fine, I'll say so, but if I'm not—if my world is turning upside-down and I need an extra dose of prayers from my friends—I'm going to share my burdens and feel the beautiful relief of having Christian friends by my side through the storm. They are there for the good times, and they are there for the bad. Just the way Christ meant them to be.

This Week: Do you have something weighing heavy on your heart? Release that burden. Christ didn't plan on us making this journey alone. Allow your fellow Christians to help you through the tough times, and do the same in return.

My Prayer to Start this Week:

Those to Remember in Prayer this Week:

MONDAY, APRIL 11

"Consider it pure joy, my brothers and sisters, whenever you face trials of many kinds, because you know that the testing of your faith produces perseverance." ~ James 1:2-3

Have you ever had one of those days when it seemed nothing went right? You couldn't say it was one of your worst days ever, since no one ended up in the hospital, but the day was definitely a bad day from the get-go. That's the way this day started.

I woke early and decided to do laundry. Doing laundry used to involve me going to our laundry room, sorting clothes and washing them at my leisure throughout the day. But that was before we lived in a motorhome for a year and sold or gave away all of our furniture, as well as our washer and dryer. Since we are in a rental home until we find a house to purchase, we haven't bought a washer and dryer. Therefore, I do my laundry at the Laundromat down the street.

Today, I didn't have too many clothes to wash, so I decided to pile them all into one of the large, commercial washers. This would have been fine, but I had forgotten about my husband's old tennis shoes in the middle of the pile. I had also forgotten that he painted the trim on the outside of the house, and that those shoes were covered with paint. As a result, when the laundry finished, nothing was clean. In fact, everything was covered with specks of white paint. And I was out of laundry detergent.

Since the detergent dispenser at the Laundromat was empty, I headed to the Wal-Mart a couple of miles away. It didn't take long to find the detergent, and I quickly headed to the front, where several employees were gathered near the cash registers. But none of them were working at a register. I asked if someone could check me out, and they explained that the self checkout system was the only thing available prior to 7:00 a.m. It was roughly 6:45 a.m. I moved to the self checkout and went from one machine to another until I determined that every machine was out of order. Finally, one of the cashiers came over and entered her code into the machine to help me scan the laundry detergent. I then selected the button to get cash back, since I'd already used all of my change at the Laundromat and needed more quarters for round two of the wash. And this is when I found out that the self checkout cash dispensing system wasn't working.

Frustrated more than I care to admit, I left Wal-Mart and went to the nearest gas station to hopefully get some cash that I could use at the coin dispensing machine at the Laundromat. The station didn't have an ATM, so I had to make a purchase to get cash back. I grabbed a pack of mints and got in line. The cashier had bloodshot eyes, and I assumed she had probably worked the entire night and was due to get off of work soon. The man in front of me, however, didn't seem to notice or care, because when her cash register locked up, and she couldn't ring up his purchase, he spouted pure venom for the world to hear and ripped the lady apart, as though she had done something wrong. Then he left all of the items on the counter and stormed out of the station.

The lady's lip trembled. She looked as upset as I'd felt before I walked in. But I was no longer upset about my day. I felt too sorry for the woman in front of me to be worried about a little paint on my clothes or a little frustration over my inability to get change at Wal-Mart. The lady immediately started apologizing for her register being down and told me she'd have it working again as soon as possible. I told her to take her time, and the machine whirred to life again in less than a minute. She rang up my mints and gave me the requested cash back so that I now had money for the Laundromat. I told her, "I hope the rest of your day is extremely blessed." And that's when the tears that had been swimming in her eyes spilled over. She thanked me and said that she needed to hear those words. Then she told me how much she appreciated my understanding.

I'd gone into that gas station probably as frustrated as that man who left the items he wanted on the counter, but I left feeling joyful. Smiling, even. The tiny problems that began my day didn't really matter. What mattered, and what I thanked God for right then, was the chance I had to give that woman, also having a rough day, a little joy. And in doing so, I experienced joy too.

This Week: If you're having "one of those days," take a moment to evaluate whether everything is as bad as it seems. Look around, and chances are you'll see someone whose day makes yours feel like a walk in the park. God gave us the natural ability to feel good when we help others, so that by helping someone else, we are essentially helping ourselves. Do what you can to lift that person's spirits, and see how your own spirits will be lifted too.

My Prayer to Start this Week:

Those to Remember in Prayer this Week:

MONDAY, APRIL 18

"There are six things the Lord hates, seven that are detestable to him: haughty eyes, a lying tongue, hands that shed innocent blood, a heart that devises wicked schemes, feet that are quick to rush into evil, a false witness who pours out lies and a person who stirs up conflict in the community." ~ Proverbs 6:16-19

I have a dear friend who is one of the most positive people I've ever met. In fact, of everyone I know, she most reminds me of the character named Clara in the movie War Room. It isn't uncommon to hear her ask if she can pray for you if you're going through a hard time. She wakes early to read her Bible and is raising her children to know the Lord and to never be ashamed of the God they serve. Her children are precious, and so is she.

So when I went to see her and found her crying, I knew something was wrong. I've seen her cry over people who have passed on. I've seen her cry over a sermon that touched her heart. But this time, she cried because someone attempted to destroy her impact on the community, ruin her reputation to her brothers and sisters in Christ, and weaken her influence over her children.

She has often admitted to going through rebellious teen years and is vocal in thanking her parents for "praying her through." She praises God for providing the forgiveness needed for anything she did in the past that didn't glorify him.

Yet an old acquaintance dug up a derogatory photo and posted it on social media, tagging my friend with something that claimed this was typical behavior. The other person wanted to break her spirit, and for a brief period, succeeded.

Clearly, the devil has lots of new opportunities to cause Christians pain, particularly through social media. Most people have something in their past that they wouldn't want put on display for the world to see. Personally, I like social media as a means of building one another up. Encouraging. Edifying. My friend often posts Bible verses and scripture on her page, and she is fine now; she forgave and moved on, still glorifying God at every opportunity.

I wonder if I could forgive that way, if someone intentionally tried to hurt me or my family, but then I realize that if I am to follow Christ's example, I will do as He did when He forgave those who put Him on the cross.

This Week: If you're on social media, post something positive each day this week.

My Prayer to Start this Week:

Those to Remember in Prayer this Week:

MONDAY, APRIL 25

"Follow God's example, therefore, as dearly loved children and walk in the way of love, just as Christ loved us and gave himself up for us as a fragrant offering and sacrifice to God." ~ Ephesians 5:1-2

Yesterday, I took Alanus and Jerry to soccer practice. Both of the boys attack each practice as though they are playing a game, and I have a lot of fun watching them…and trying to remember when I had that much energy. But because of their aggressive running and kicking on the field, or maybe because he didn't stretch before he practiced, Alanus strained his groin.

I noticed he seemed to be favoring his right leg as we left the field, but when I asked him about it, he said he was fine. However, by the time we got home, he'd decided he wasn't fine after all, and he decided to self-diagnose the situation.

As we entered the house, he stopped walking, fell flat on his back and said, "It's a cramp. This is what I'm supposed to do." Then Jerry said, "I know what to do too," and proceeded to yank Alanus' foot back in an effort to relieve the cramp.

I managed to keep from laughing, because I knew where they learned "what to do." Rene, their Daddy and our oldest son, coaches football. The boys had obviously seen the high school players fall on their back and have their foot yanked to relieve cramps on the field on Friday nights.

Alanus is fine now, but the scene reminded me how much children learn from what they see. The boys saw the way to treat a cramp, and so they banked on that knowledge.

Naturally, J.R. and I found a lot of humor in their actions; however, I also find plenty of comfort in the fact that they are imitators of the adults in their world. You see, their world is surrounded by adults and teens that are steadfastly following Christ. The boys know to pray when something isn't going well, or when it is, because they see their parents and friends praying. They also know that Jesus loves them, and that their parents and family love them too…because they see the proof of that love every day.

In the verse above, we are told to follow God's example. That's even more important when we realize how many may follow our example. Little eyes are watching and learning and imitating. Make sure when they remember "what to do" in a given situation, the things they learned from you will be done through Christ.

This Week: Help a child memorize Philippians 4:13.

My Prayer to Start this Week:

Those to Remember in Prayer this Week:

MONDAY, MAY 2

"So we fix our eyes not on what is seen, but on what is unseen, since what is seen is temporary, but what is unseen is eternal." ~ 2 Corinthians 4:18

As a writer, I'm always fascinated by quotes from notable authors. Recently, I read the following quote by James Patterson:

"Focus on the story, not the sentence."

Undoubtedly great advice for writers, who will often get so wrapped up in every word of a sentence or one small section of the book that we lose sight of the big picture. But our readers are interested in the big picture, what is important and what makes the book a bestseller. It's the story that sells books, not a sentence.

His advice also applies to our spiritual lives. It's so easy to get wrapped up in what is happening in our world right now and lose sight of the big picture. I can think of the list of errands that I have to do today, of the health issues going on in my life or my family members' lives, of the upcoming deadline, of the bills that need to be paid, of the house that needs to be cleaned, of the to-do list that is ever growing. Financial burdens, health issues, familial struggles…so many things grab our focus and pull our attention away from the One who can put all of that to ease, the One who can provide our peace.

I've found that as I age, it seems more difficult for the devil to steal my joy. For example, over the past week, my son's motorcycle was stolen from his garage at his home, a young woman's car was broken into and her purse stolen in the parking lot of our business, and I sliced my finger open trying to help her clean up the broken glass from the busted window. Additionally, our oldest son had planned to close on his house today but the contractor backed out last night. So many things that could claim my focus and remove my mind from Christ. So many things that could cause me to try to fix it all myself, instead of turning it over to the One in control.

This morning, as I discussed the past week with our children, I was amazed that I'm at peace. Yes, we've had a tough week, but God has got this. He's got everything. And as long as we remember to focus on the story instead of the sentence, we'll be just fine. Nothing is going to steal my joy. This world is not my home.

This Week: Take the top two things attempting to steal your joy and ask God to help you focus on the story instead of the sentence. Tell yourself, "He's got this!" and then hand it over to Him.

My Prayer to Start this Week:

Those to Remember in Prayer this Week:

MONDAY, MAY 9

"But God demonstrates his own love for us in this: While we were still sinners, Christ died for us." ~ Romans 5:8

We have a post office box that we use for our personal mail. The post office is located in the center of town and is a reminder of the small Southern community where we live, because I rarely enter the building that I don't see at least one familiar face. And since I often check our mail fairly early in the morning, most people are still happy with the new day. I'm often greeted with smiles and a "Good Morning" or two. Honestly, that trip to the post office is a great way to lift my spirits as I start my day.

So this morning, as I went to check our box, I said, "Good Morning," a couple of times and answered a few people with an "I'm fine." But as I retrieved my mail from my box, I listened to another exchange in the post office.

A woman asked a gentleman how he was doing, and his answer was one I haven't heard before. He said with a broad smile:

"Better than I deserve."

Wow. He nailed it, not only for himself, but for all of us. Whether we are in the best shape of our life…or not. Whether we are having a great day…or not. Whether our bank account has lots of zeroes at the end of each number…or not. Whether we have a large, loving family…or not.

No matter our current circumstance, we are doing...better than we deserve.

How can I say that with certainty? Because we are here because Someone gave His very life to save us. We have the glorious opportunity of life after death because of His sacrifice. Do we deserve such a sacrifice? No. Do we deserve such a gift? No. Is there anything we could ever do to earn it on our own? No way.

Yet Christ died for us, even though we can never be, "good enough." Even though we can never repay our debt. Even though we do things that may shame Him, hurt Him, He offers us salvation for our souls.

How are we doing?

Better than we deserve.

This Week: I've written another devotion where I encourage you to answer to, "How are you doing?" with, "I'm blessed." This week, I am going to encourage you to respond with a different answer: "Better than I deserve." It's a beautiful, true statement...praise God!

My Prayer to Start this Week:

Those to Remember in Prayer this Week:

MONDAY, MAY 16

"But you are a chosen people, a royal priesthood, a holy nation, God's special possession, that you may declare the praises of him who called you out of darkness into his wonderful light." ~ *1 Peter 2:9*

With J.R.'s business, we often travel to other gymnastics and tumbling facilities. Last night, I needed to drive to another business to pick up something for him, since he had to work late. I do this often, and I usually enjoy the chance to visit a different place and meet new people, make new friends. But last night, my trip to the other gym didn't go as planned.

Shortly before I arrived, a mother and her daughter left the building after the child's tumbling class ended. I now know that the parents are going through a custody battle over the daughter, and the husband/dad was waiting in the parking lot for a confrontation. He began punching the mother, and on the last punch, he missed his ex-wife and hit his daughter. The police were called and reports filed.

The situation was horrible and so very, very sad, but what was the most shocking to me was the way the children in and around the gym reacted to the physical abuse in the parking lot, as though this was something completely…normal.

Honestly, they were more concerned with getting back to their tumbling than what had occurred outside. And when they said anything about it, they simply shrugged as though that's the way things are.

Are things that way nowadays? Is that what children are growing up to see as normal? I understand that there is violence in the world, but I didn't realize that, in many children's lives, that is the norm.

Oddly enough, I recently had a discussion with a young newlywed who was describing her marriage and her husband's Christian family as compared to her own. She'd grown up in an extremely dysfunctional, very broken home; he, on the other hand, grew up surrounded by love and a kind of support that she didn't realize existed. When she spoke about the difference, it was with tears streaming down her cheeks. "I never realize something like this could be normal."

My heart broke for the family that fought last night. My heart broke for the children in that gym who didn't realize that the abuse shouldn't be typical. And my heart broke for the young woman so used to neglect that she was shell-shocked by true unconditional love, the kind of love that she now knows exists, not only from her husband, but more importantly by her Heavenly Father.

Yes, the "normal" in many individuals' lives isn't the ideal situation. But Christ calls us out of the darkness and into His glorious light. We can be the light to others who aren't even aware a light exists.

This Week: Pay attention to those who have a different interpretation of "normal." Show them the light of Christ, with a smile, with your words, with a touch. Change the "normal" in their world.

My Prayer to Start this Week:

Those to Remember in Prayer this Week:

MONDAY, MAY 23

"Declare his glory among the nations, his marvelous deeds among all peoples." ~ 1 Chronicles 16:24

Our life group, or small group Bible study, often shares needs with each other. These may be needs of members of the group, or sometimes needs of individuals that we hear about at work, in our community or at school.

Tonight, I sent a note to the life group that began like this:

Hello, Amazing Life Group!
We have a wonderful opportunity to serve :)

I then informed them about a young lady needing help and identified the items the life group members could bring next Sunday to send a care package her way.

Barely ten minutes later, I received a message from Craig Humphrey. Craig became a part of our life group a few years ago and then moved to Florida. But he is still a part of the group, and he's always the first to respond when someone needs help. Quite honestly, he has a huge heart and an astronomical love of serving others. When he did live locally and was able to attend our Bible studies, he never failed to bring a home-cooked dish to the meeting. We all share a meal each week, but my usual contribution is something I can pick up quickly, such as pizzas or chicken fingers. Craig, on the other hand, would bring unique dishes he thought we would enjoy, and he'd spend his Sunday afternoon cooking, while I typically spent my time between church services napping (did I mention how easy it is to pick up those pizzas or chicken fingers?).

Tonight, when I received that message informing me that he wanted to send a check to help the young lady, I was struck by the beauty of serving others, particularly when you see someone do it with such eagerness. And I understood that Craig's service wasn't merely when he would contribute toward a need that had been brought to the group; he also served each of us every week when he came to Bible study when he prepared a special dish.

I enjoy serving; I do. But after looking at the way Craig serves, I see that I often take the easy way out, when a little time would allow me to experience another level of joy, serving, even when the activity isn't deemed "serving". What a concept, to merely look for what you can do for others, whether they are in need, or not. And how Christ-like, to figure that out and follow through.

I think for our next life group, I'll actually cook.

This Week: Make two pots of soup of chili, one for you and the other for your neighbor or friend. Experience the joy of serving.

My Prayer to Start this Week:

Those to Remember in Prayer this Week:

MONDAY, MAY 30

"I have told you these things, so that in me you may have peace. In this world you will have trouble. But take heart! I have overcome the world." John 16:33

A young couple recently came to look at our home for sale. We spent some time going through the house and allowing me to answer their questions, and then they wanted to go outside and view the land. When they arrived at the house, the weather was pleasant, with a nice, cool breeze and the sun shining; however, by the time we toured the inside of the home and then went outside, the sky had darkened. The breeze had turned into a windy bluster. Leaves, and even a few small branches, were pushed from the trees and fluttered to the ground.

Amazed at the quick change, we commented on how quickly the weather seems to alter in this part of Alabama. And then, while we watched, rain swiftly coated the homes across the street, so that we had to dash inside, because we could literally see it crossing the street and heading to our property.

Our lives are often similar to those swift, summer storms. We can feel the changing winds, see the darkening skies of trouble coming, and then, inevitably, the storm comes. Some storms of life happen so quickly, we aren't prepared, and we can't get inside quickly enough. The unexpected passing of a loved one, for example. Other storms come slowly and are often even more painful because of the increased passage of time. Watching my grandmother suffer through Alzheimer's, seeing her disappear a little more each day, proved to be a painful, slow storm.

In Matthew 7, Jesus talks about two builders, one who built his house on the rock and the other who built his home on the sand. My grandchildren love singing the story of the house that went, "Splat!" As a child, that was my main focus of the story too; one house stood firm, the other tumbled down. But as an adult, I look at the story differently. Both houses, the one on the rock and the one on the sand, were hit with storms. And whether we have our faith in Christ or not, we will have troubles in the life. That's a given; this world is not perfect, by any means. But now, when we see that rain coming, when we feel the winds changing, we know that with Him as our foundation, our house isn't going anywhere. He is our rock. Praise God!

This Week: Sing, "The Wise Man Built his House Upon the Rock" with a child.

My Prayer to Start this Week:

Those to Remember in Prayer this Week:

MONDAY, JUNE 6

"The Lord God said, 'It is not good for the man to be alone. I will make a helper suitable for him.'" ~ Genesis 2:18

"He who finds a wife finds what is good and receives favor from the Lord.." ~ Proverbs 18:22

Therefore I tell you, whatever you ask for in prayer, believe that you have received it, and it will be yours." ~ Mark 11:24

Each morning, J.R. and I start our day by reading devotions and praying together. Our prayers always vary somewhat based on what is going on in our life, but a portion remains the same: we pray for our children, for their mates, for our grandchildren and for the grandchildren to come. We want God to know that our family is a priority, and we pray for their spiritual health and their physical health.

When I say that we pray for our children's mates, I think it's important to also mention that we began praying for our daughters-in-law before they were even born. I've told the girls that, that we prayed for them way before they ever met our sons. We know the value of a Godly mate. I know that our marriage grows stronger when we grow closer to Christ together. We wanted that for our children too, and before we even met our daughters-in-law, we prayed:

"God, please bless the girls that You have planned for our sons. Bring them up to know You and to love You, prepare them to be the Godly wives that will nurture the marriage they will have with Rene and Kaleb. Take care of them as they grow. Let them have faith in their future with You, and with the men who will love them as Christ loves the church."

I know that God heard those prayers. I know that He hears our prayers for them still. And now, he hears the prayers for the future mates of our grandchildren. I believe it is important to ask God to watch after those who will have such a very important role in our family, even if we haven't met...even if they haven't been born. He knows what is to come, and He hears our prayers for relationships in the present...and in the future.

This Week: Search for the song, "Somewhere in the World," by Wayne Watson. It's beautiful, and it discusses prayers for a child's future mate. Then pray for your children and for their mates, whether your child is thirty-two...or two. Praise God that He answers prayers for today...and for the tomorrows yet to come!

My Prayer to Start this Week:

Those to Remember in Prayer this Week:

MONDAY, JUNE 13

"In a large house there are articles not only of gold and silver, but also of wood and clay; some are for special purposes and some for common use. Those who cleanse themselves from the latter will be instruments for special purposes, made holy, useful to the Master and prepared to do any good work." ~ 2 Timothy 2:20-21

Throughout my life, I've had times where I've doubted my usefulness to God. These questions whispered in the back of my mind:

"Am I good enough for God?"

"Why should I even try, if I'm so useless to Him with my endless ability to sin?"

In my late high school years and throughout my years of college, that last question plagued my soul. I didn't like myself much, and I was jealous of those who appeared to have it all together who seemed so confident in their life and in their faith. It took years, and most definitely a true understanding of God's grace, to see the beauty of God's gift of salvation, of Christ's sacrifice on the cross for my sin. Now I have answers:

"Am I good enough for God?" No, no one is, but God's grace covers over our imperfection.

"Why should I even try, if I'm so useless to Him with my endless ability to sin?" Because God doesn't see me as useless. He looks

at me and sees someone His Son was willing to die for. He looks at me and sees His child.

And any time I start to think I can't be useful to God, I remember David, the man after God's own heart, and recall that he was, at one of his low points in life, an adulterer and a murderer. In fact, at their low points...Noah got drunk, Jacob lied, Moses stuttered, Rahab was a prostitute, Jonah ran from God, Peter denied Christ, and Jesus' own disciples fell asleep while praying.

If God can use them, He can use me.

This Week: Try to go the next seven days without saying, "I can't."

My Prayer to Start this Week:

Those to Remember in Prayer this Week:

MONDAY, JUNE 20

"So you also must be ready, because the Son of Man will come at an hour when you do not expect him." ~ Matthew 24:44

A couple of months ago, a friend told me about a man who needed a ride to church each week. He'd suffered a stroke and could no longer drive. He's also lost the ability to think as clearly as he did before, with his speech impaired. Walking takes a lot of concentration.

So now, each week, we pick Jeff up and take him to church. I can't tell you what a blessing it is to see how excited he is to go to worship. I've been able to tell that it makes him happy by the bright smile he displays when we arrive at the building. But I really saw the excitement one week when my husband was out of town, and I went to pick Jeff up on my own.

J.R. usually walks to the door to get Jeff, but this time, I made my way up the sidewalk to knock on the door of his mother's home (he hasn't been able to live independently since the stroke). As I neared the door, I heard him yell to his mother, "They're ready! They're ready!" He honestly sounded like a child on Christmas morning, and it was all I could do not to cry. He was thrilled to be going to church, something that I often take for granted. Obviously, when Jeff yelled, "They're ready!" he meant "They're here!" But his words could've also meant something else, that we *are* ready. Ready for our Lord. In sharing his excitement, Jeff sparked mine as well, reminding me that not only should we be "here," but we should also be "ready."

When Christ comes, I want to yell like Jeff. "We're ready!"

This Week: Find someone who needs a ride to church and offer to take him or her along. You'll be blessed beyond measure!

My Prayer to Start this Week:

Those to Remember in Prayer this Week:

MONDAY, JUNE 27

"Devote yourselves to prayer, being watchful and thankful." ~
Colossians 4:2

A typical text between me and either of our sons:

Me: Hey, how is everything going?
Him: Fine.
Me: Work okay?
Him: Yes, going good.
Me: Everything else okay?
Him: Yes, fine.
Me: Love you.
Him: Love you too.

The communication is there, but neither of us can hear the other's tone. We also don't convey near as much as we would if we were in person or even talking on the phone.

I don't have a problem with texting. In fact, in many cases, I'm sure I can get in touch with the kids much easier because they might be able to send a quick text at a time when they aren't able to carry on a long conversation.

But that doesn't mean that I don't long for a nice, lengthy conversation whenever the opportunity arises. Then I can actually hear it in their voices that they're doing okay, or that they aren't. There's just something different about actually talking to one another, taking time to describe what is going on in each other's world and how we are dealing with life in general.

When I compare that scenario to my prayer life, I wonder if I'm not sometimes putting myself in a text-only relationship with my Heavenly Father. Yes, I pray before meals. Often I pray at other times throughout the day too. But am I taking every opportunity I can to carry on a lengthy conversation with my Lord? We're commanded to pray continually (1 Thessalonians 5:17). Now I don't think that means spend every minute in prayer, but "continually" would seem to convey that God wants to hear from us on a regular basis, throughout our day, instead of merely before bed and before meals…or when times are really bad.

At times of struggle—sickness, financial troubles, relationship woes—then, it's easy to break out those long, begging prayers where we talk and talk and talk to God about what we need to remedy the situation. But what if we were praying with that kind of depth all of the time? If I appreciate those conversations with my children, how much more would my Lord and Savior appreciate hearing from me, the one He created?

If we keep that prayer line open, talking to Him the way He intended, then it'd be much easier to have prayer the way God intended, as our first response, rather than our last resort.

This Week: Estimate the number of times you pray each day. Double that number, and see how much closer you feel to your Lord. Increase the length of your prayers too—He gives us the ability to talk to Him at all times. Don't waste that golden opportunity to share your day, every day, with Him.

My Prayer to Start this Week:

Those to Remember in Prayer this Week:

MONDAY, JULY 4

"Therefore, as we have opportunity, let us do good to all people, especially to those who belong to the family of believers."
Galatians 6:10

Last week, I started feeling poorly. My throat was scratchy, and my head ached. I thought I was getting my annual "summer cold" and ignored it, thinking after a few days, it'd go away as usual. But a week passed, and one day of running a fever slipped in the middle, and then I couldn't swallow at all, so I headed to the doctor.

Sure enough, I had a throat infection. Feeling terrible, I sat in my assigned room awaiting two shots (a steroid and an antibiotic) and the results of the throat swabbing (always loads of fun, when I gag for the nurse). But as I sat there listening to the music playing through the speakers, I recognized the song as one of my favorite Christian contemporary tunes. I also realized that Christian music had played the entire time I'd been in the office. Since I listen to the contemporary Christian station in my car, I hadn't noticed that the songs continued as I entered. However, I immediately knew I was in the right doctor's office and that everything was going to be okay. I also made a conscious decision to always come to this particular urgent care facility when I am feeling poorly.

Likewise, my favorite grocery store is the one that is owned by a local family...and plays Christian music for customers. And I also frequently shop at Hobby Lobby because I know the morals of the owners of the chain, and I know I'll hear spiritually themed music as I make my purchases.

I've noticed over the years that I pay attention to stores that are owned by Christians and that obviously represent values. I also pay attention when a place of business treats me the way Christ would treat others. For example, I use a particular dry cleaning place in town because of something that happened one of the first times that I had them dry clean my laundry. I had a pair of J.R.'s dress pants in the clothes to be cleaned. When I picked up the laundry, the woman handed me my receipt, which had a ten-dollar bill attached to the paper slip. I asked about the money, and she let me know that J.R. had left it in the pocket of his pants.

I've never been to another dry cleaners.

In the verse above, we are told to do good to others, especially those who believe. If we determine that a place or person is a believer, we should do our best to support that business/person/activity.

This Week: Pay attention to your choices of places to shop, eat or meet. If you know that God is at the helm of a business or organization, support those places first. And if a Christian movie is playing at your local theater, by all means, go see the film. Encourage your church family to join you! Support those of the household of faith. And if you own a business, let the world know that God is your true CEO.

My Prayer to Start this Week:

Those to Remember in Prayer this Week:

MONDAY, JULY 11

"I the Lord do not change." ~ Malachi 3:6

We have always traveled, even before our job required the time on the road. Because J.R. is from Baton Rouge and I'm from a tiny town in North Alabama (Glencoe, a town quite similar to the fictional town of Claremont in my fictional series), we have always had family that lived a good distance away. Add that to the fact that we enjoy camping and you'll understand we've stayed on the go since we were first married.

So Rene and Kaleb have been accustomed to long rides in the car since they were born. They had no problem with traveling long distances to spend time together or to see family members. But if we were traveling over the weekend, we would find a church in the vicinity of our vacation spot and attend the services. Before we would even enter the church parking lot, both boys began pleading their cases. "Do we have to go to class?" "I don't want to go to a new class." "We won't know anyone in our class." "If we have to go, can we go together, to the same one?"

Typically, J.R. and I walked with them to find their classroom and stood nearby while they peeked inside. We never made them attend; they could sit with us in the auditorium if they didn't feel comfortable. But often they would decide to be with other kids their age rather than spend their time in a large auditorium with a bunch of adults.

The boys weren't thrilled when we'd move either; again, because of our jobs, we've lived in several places over the years. I can't remember a time when the boys weren't disheartened about the change—making new friends, attending a new school, and leaving their old friends behind.

I didn't admit it to the boys at the time, but I was also sad with each move. Starting over isn't fun. New community. New church. New schools for the kids. New friends. Leaving my comfort zone…again.

But life is full of changes, isn't it? There will always be a "first" for each aspect of our life. First day of elementary school, then middle school and then high school. First date. First job interview. First child. Each first equates to another moment of change in our world. And typically, no one likes change.

Isn't it refreshing to know that there is One constant that we can count on. One permanent that we can hold on to when the going gets tough.

I the Lord do not change.

Praise God that He provides a sound stability in an ever-changing, often troubling world. The calm in our storm. The peace in our frustration. The Way. The Truth. The Life.

This Week: Write down your last two addresses, the names of two friends who've moved or who you've moved away from and the names of the last two family members who have passed on to their reward. Think of all of the changes that occurred with each of the items you've written on the page. Thank God that, in a world that requires constant adjustment, He remains steady and strong. He. Does. Not. Change.

My Prayer to Start this Week:

Those to Remember in Prayer this Week:

MONDAY, JULY 18

"Truthful lips endure forever, but a lying tongue lasts only a moment." ~ Proverbs 12:19

While J.R. and I were visiting with a group of friends recently, one of the men, a natural storyteller, made this statement:

"Nowadays, you can't attempt to tell a lie, because the minute you start, someone pulls out their smart phone and starts checking your facts."

His comment was made jokingly, but it made me think about the truth of his statement, not so much that people have the ability to verify what we have said but that, when telling a non-truth, we are more worried about the possibility of being exposed by our peers than the fact that God sees every word, knows every thought, and doesn't need the Internet to verify fact versus fiction.

Our oldest son asked a question in a recent sermon that resonated with me: "What if you had a speech bubble above your head throughout the day, the kind of thing you see above cartoon characters' heads in comic strips to show what they're thinking, except this one showed all of your thoughts, spoken and unspoken. Would you want the rest of the world to see your every thought?"

Obviously, God knows that we aren't perfect. In fact, if we look at some of the most well-known Biblical heroes, we see their lies exposed: Abraham lied when he said Sarah was his sister, rather than his wife, and Samson lied when he first told Delilah the secret of his strength. But God knew their hearts (1 Samuel 16:7) and, praise God, He knows ours. He knows when we are repentant of our lies, and of our unpure thoughts, but He also doesn't expect us to continue, simply because of His grace (Romans 6).

This Week: Imagine a cartoon speech bubble above your head, showing the world what God already knows. Let those words be something He would be proud of, something you would be unashamed of.

My Prayer to Start this Week:

Those to Remember in Prayer this Week:

MONDAY, JULY 25

"See to it, brothers and sisters, that none of you has a sinful, unbelieving heart that turns away from the living God. But encourage one another daily, as long as it is called "Today," so that none of you may be hardened by sin's deceitfulness." ~ Hebrews 3:12-13

The house where we currently live is across the street from a high school football field. Since my oldest son coaches football at the high school, the proximity to the field has been extremely convenient. Not only can we walk across the street to see him coach his team on Friday nights, but we're also a convenient go-to spot for the grandboys when their Daddy has practice each afternoon.

However, when the football team isn't practicing, the drum line takes over. Now I love the drum line on Friday night, but each day when I'm trying to write, their ba-da-bum-bum-bum can get quite intense. We moved here three months ago, and I'd say for the first month and a half, I simply couldn't write while the drums beat across the street. Then, all of a sudden, I could write, regardless of the fact that they seem to get even louder as the season goes on.

I'm sure my adjustment to the sound was a gradual process, but I didn't even realize that it was happening, which made me think of other times in life where people adapt to sounds or situations. For example, when J.R. and I took our cross-country motorcycle trip, we passed chicken plants with a smell that hurt the back of my throat, yet I would see people in their yards near the plant, kids playing basketball outside within a mile of the stench. Likewise, we stayed in a campground where a train seemed to blast right through the middle of the place every night, and all of the locals kept sleeping.

The point I am making is this: if you are around something enough, it becomes your version of normal. You eventually become numb to the uncomfortableness of the situation, and you can continue as if everything is a-okay.

Now think of that illustration when applied to your spiritual life, or more accurately, your sinful life. At first, you'll hear or see something that you know isn't Godly and you cringe inside. Maybe it's a curse word. A bad movie. A dirty joke. A place where you aren't comfortable and wouldn't want to be seen by your Christian friends. After a while, it stops bothering you as much. And then you aren't bothered at all. You've become numb to the sin.

Like stated in the verse above, we can become "hardened" to the sin. That word as used in the verse comes from the Greek word *callus*, which is where we get the word callous. A callous, that hardened bit of skin that forms from constant use, is known for being tough, difficult to get rid of, and obtained slowly, over time. However, I've seen many gymnasts cut callouses away. And I've had a few of my own that, over time, I removed. You can get rid of that tough, hardened skin, just as you can soften your heart again to sin. How? By turning away from the sin and to the One who gave you the ability to wince when you neared that danger. Next time you feel yourself cringing at where you are, what you're hearing or what you're about to do, remember the pain of cutting a callous away—and stop this one before it starts.

This Week: Take inventory of the things that once made you cringe and now no longer create the same effect. If a callous has formed, cut it away!

My Prayer to Start this Week:

Those to Remember in Prayer this Week:

MONDAY, AUGUST 1

"Moses said to the Lord, "Pardon your servant, Lord. I have never been eloquent, neither in the past nor since you have spoken to your servant. I am slow of speech and tongue." ~ Exodus 4:10

I've been praying for my nephew this week. He received a football scholarship and moved away from home to play for the team and begin his college studies, and I know that it's always difficult when you start something new. We've had a lot of "new beginnings" in our family this year: our youngest son graduated ministry school, got married and began a new job three hours away. Our oldest son and daughter-in-law learned they are expecting our first granddaughter, due in December. Although they have our two oldest grandsons, they've never had a baby, so even though Naomi will be their third child; she definitely brings a new experience to the table.

New beginnings are exciting, but often scary. There is a fear of the unknown, a trepidation involved when you aren't sure you're prepared for what is to come. In the verse above, Moses begs God to change His mind about sending him to Egypt to speak on behalf of the Israelites. This request had been immediately preceded by God changing Moses' staff into a snake and then converting it to a staff again, as well as causing Moses' hand to become leprous and then healing the disease while Moses watched. Moses had no reason to think that God would ask him to do anything that wouldn't be accompanied by God's help.

Yet he begged not to go.

Throughout life, we all experience some or all of the following: new job, new school, addition of a baby, loss of the loved one who was the "glue" that held the family intact, moving to another city, your child moving away for college, a marriage, a separation or divorce. All of these can be traumatic and life-changing.

But, as Moses learned, God doesn't give you more than you can handle, as long as you have Him by your side. Pray as you go through life's abundance of new beginnings and ever-changing situations. Pray for God to guide your path, and remember that He is in control.

This Week: It's August. You probably know someone who has: married over the summer, begun a new job or started at a new school. Say a special prayer for that person or persons today, that they will trust in God and find courage in the new beginning knowing He is with them for the journey. And if you're the one starting something new, pray for God to lift your spirits, remove the trepidation and bless your new endeavor.

Note: If you enjoy these devotions, please take a look at www.MondayswithJesus.com to pre-order Mondays with Jesus 2017. You can purchase autographed, personalized copies for $9.99, the same price the book sells in stores, with free U.S. shipping ☺ I'd love to share my love of the Lord with you, your friends and relatives next year and hope that you'll see this book as an affordable option for your holiday gift-giving. Blessings always, Renee

My Prayer to Start this Week:

Those to Remember in Prayer this Week:

MONDAY, AUGUST 8

"Whoever claims to live in him must live as Jesus did." ~ 1 John 2:6

It's August, which in Northern Alabama means it's hot. Lately, the temperature in the afternoon has hovered anywhere between ninety and a hundred degrees. Because of this, J.R. usually cuts the grass at our business and at our home in the afternoon, but today, other commitments wouldn't allow him to wait, and he started midday.

After he had been at our gym for longer than usual, I decided to drive over and bring him a bottle of water. I was surprised when I arrived at the gym to find that he'd finished the grass and, instead of driving home to start on our yard, he'd moved to the community church next door and proceeded to cut their grass. I have no idea whether he has been cutting the grass there all summer or whether this was the first time, but he's never mentioned it. I'm sure he wouldn't have mentioned it today if I hadn't driven there and seen his act of service. Later, he cut our grass at home while I started cooking dinner. After a while, when the task took longer than usual, I checked outside to find that our grass was cut...and he'd moved on to the neighbor's yard.

I often pray to be Christ-like. I ask for God to help me see needs and to serve others the way He wants me to. Today, I witnessed my husband serving others, and my heart melted. I love him always, but my love for him today moved me to tears, and I realized that it's very easy to love someone when they are imitating Christ.

This Week: Serve someone in secret. As J.R. did, do something without being asked, without expecting anything in return. My sweet Cajun doesn't know I'm writing a devotion about him right now. But what is really wonderful is that I asked God to put a thought-provoking devotion on my heart today...and He sent me to the gym with that water bottle.

My Prayer to Start this Week:

Those to Remember in Prayer this Week:

MONDAY, AUGUST 15

"And what more shall I say? I do not have time to tell about Gideon, Barak, Samson and Jephthah, about David and Samuel and the prophets, who through faith conquered kingdoms, administered justice, and gained what was promised; who shut the mouths of lions, quenched the fury of the flames, and escaped the edge of the sword; whose weakness was turned to strength; and who became powerful in battle and routed foreign armies. Women received back their dead, raised to life again. There were others who were tortured, refusing to be released so that they might gain an even better resurrection. Some faced jeers and flogging, and even chains and imprisonment. They were put to death by stoning; they were sawed in two; they were killed by the sword. They went about in sheepskins and goatskins, destitute, persecuted and mistreated—the world was not worthy of them. They wandered in deserts and mountains, living in caves and in holes in the ground. These were all commended for their faith, yet none of them received what had been promised, since God had planned something better for us so that only together with us would they be made perfect." ~ Hebrews 11:32-40

Yesterday, our oldest son Rene preached a sermon about the famed chapter of faith, Hebrews 11. He's been teaching a series on Hebrews, and I had looked forward to one of my favorite chapters of the Bible. Oddly enough, after so many years of reading this scripture, I had inadvertently missed a key portion of the text, and his interpretation allowed me to see it in a different light.

Throughout the chapter, many are mentioned and acknowledged for what they did "by faith," as well as what they received "by faith." But in my previous readings I had only concentrated on the positive outcomes. Abraham went to offer Isaac as a sacrifice, but God provided another sacrifice. The Israelites crossed the Red Sea, but the Egyptians that followed drowned. Rehab lived when she welcomed the spies, while those who were disobedient died. All of these go along with the thinking, "If you have faith, the result will be positive."

However, then comes the remainder of the chapter, when we learn that some of the faithful were tortured. Stoned to death. Sawed in two. Killed by the sword. Living "by faith" didn't automatically give them a green light to a trouble-free life. Far from it. But, as my preacher often says, "God never promised smooth sailing; He promised a safe landing."

We all know (or are) those who seem to be dealt more than their fair share of trouble in life. Financial stresses. Familial struggles. Loss of health. Or those painful piercings of the heart when you lose a loved one—a friend, a parent, a spouse, a child. I have friends who have seen almost all of those tragedies, yet they remain faithful, like those listed at the end of that chapter in Hebrews. Why? Because their faith assures them that, as the last verse of the chapter states, God has planned something better.

This Week: Undoubtedly, you know someone who has recently experienced one of more of these tragedies—financial struggles, deterioration in health, loss of a loved one. Send them a reminder today that, no matter the struggles and pain of life in this world, God promises a safe landing...safe in the arms of our Savior. Praise be to God for the knowledge of a safe landing.

My Prayer to Start this Week:

Those to Remember in Prayer this Week:

MONDAY, AUGUST 22

*"Why do you look at the speck of sawdust in your brother's eye
and pay no attention to the plank in your own eye?" Luke 6:41*

When J.R. and I lived in Atlanta in the early nineties, our
church encouraged the congregation to purchase an audio version
of the Bible on cassette tapes (yes, it was that long ago) and listen
to the Bible as we traveled throughout the year. We purchased the
"dramatized" version, which had unique voices for the Biblical
men and women, as well as background sounds to further
emphasize each scene. I loved listening to the Word and actually
feeling as if I were there, hearing the apostles and Christ. The
crucifixion scene rocked me to the core, as did the scene where
God spoke to Moses at the burning bush.

One scene, however, caused me to look at the way I read the
Bible differently. It was the scene that included Luke 6:41, where
Christ asks about the sawdust in our brother's eye and the plank in
our own eye. On the dramatized version, Christ laughed as he
asked the question.

Christ? Laughing? Christ came to earth to live as a man, and
undoubtedly, his time on earth would have involved laughter. Now
I can't read that verse without hearing the actor who portrayed
Christ's voice on the tape laughing as he asked the question.

I wonder how often God finds humor in what we say or do. He
is our heavenly Father, and as such, He would see us doing things

that we should think twice about and might find the humor in it, the way Christ may have found humor when comparing the speck to the plank with regards to those judging others.

As a parent of boys, I was blessed to often find humor in situations rather than letting them cause me to get angry or upset. On one occasion, for example, Kaleb borrowed our business car while his car was in the shop for repair. He took the tiny Smart car with our logo on the outside to college for a week. While he was there, we received a call at our business from a gentleman in the town where Kaleb attended school.

"I just thought you would want to know that your employee is driving your car on the sidewalk at the University here, and something should be done about it."

The fellow didn't know that the "employee" was actually our youngest son. And the car is tiny, as I mentioned before, but Kaleb shouldn't have taken it for a ride on the sidewalk, even if it easily fit within the concrete parameters.

I called Kaleb and asked him how everything was going at school and with the car. I got a predictable, "Everything's fine, Mom." And then I asked if he'd happened to take the car on the sidewalk. Silence echoed through the line. I could have gotten mad, but I knew no harm had been done. No one had been injured, and only one man had apparently thought enough of his actions to call the number printed across the side of the car. So I laughed. And I told Kaleb that we would appreciate it if he could keep the car on the road, especially since our business name and number were plastered all over the sides.

I wonder how often I do something that is equivalent in my Lord's eyes as driving a car on the sidewalk. How often do I know that the decision I'm making could end up getting me into trouble…and I go ahead full steam anyway? Does Christ shake His heavenly head and laugh, pronouncing that I should know better and that I would learn my lesson soon? If so, I'm afraid He's probably had to do that on my behalf more times than I'd care to admit.

This Week: When you're tempted to do something that might cause Heavenly laughter from above, take a second to evaluate whether you really want to proceed. And if you do plunge ahead and receive the repercussions of your actions, thank the Heavenly Father that He may actually have found humor in you.

My Prayer to Start this Week:

Those to Remember in Prayer this Week:

MONDAY, AUGUST 29

"When that day comes, you will cry out for relief from the king you have chosen, but the Lord will not answer you in that day." ~ *1 Samuel 8:18*

Our van is approaching two hundred thousand miles. This is not uncommon for one of our vehicles; our two previous automobiles made it to nearly four hundred thousand miles and three hundred thousand miles. We basically drive a vehicle until it refuses to go. So it didn't surprise me when the wipers stopped working during a thunderstorm. As expected, visibility went from slim to nil in a matter of seconds, and the particular road that I traveled didn't have a shoulder where I could safely pull the car to the side.

I did the only thing I could do: I prayed, "Please God, keep me safe. And please let the wipers start working again."

After only a moment, the wipers sprang to life, beating at high speed, fiercely swiping the water away so that I could see again. And eventually, the rain stopped. But my wipers didn't. They remained on high gear, and even when I switched them off, they kept going, scraping against the now-dry window and screeching as they moved. Seeing more storm clouds ahead, I didn't ask God for another favor to turn the wipers off; I simply endured the noise until, as I suspected, the rain started again, and I was grateful to have working wipers.

I've heard the saying, "Be careful what you wish for." I think it would also apply to, "Be careful what you pray for." I prayed for those wipers to work, and God granted my request.

I think about times when God granted requests in the Bible, and then when things didn't end up exactly like the requestors wanted, they weren't so happy with God. The Israelites, for example, when they asked for a king, and God granted their request. God knew how that would end up, of course; He even told them! Yet they still wanted an earthly king, choosing the authority of a man over the authority of God.

The windshield wipers are one tiny example of a prayer answered with "Yes," that didn't turn out quite like expected. Other bigger prayers were requests for jobs that ended up taking me away from my children, requests for things I really didn't need that took my focus off of God, requests for situations to be resolved a certain way when another end result would have been much better.

Prayer is a powerful thing. God plans on us using it and using it often, but we should never take the privilege lightly. And if we get what we ask for, by all means, we shouldn't complain.

This Week: Discuss with your spouse, parent, child or friend a time when God granted something you requested in prayer. Share the experience, good or bad, of God saying, "Yes!"

My Prayer to Start this Week:

Those to Remember in Prayer this Week:

MONDAY, SEPTEMBER 5

"Rejoice always, pray continually, give thanks in all circumstances; for this is God's will for you in Christ Jesus." ~ 1 Thessalonians 5:16-18

J.R and I just finished a "21 Days of Prayer" event hosted by our youngest son Kaleb's church. During the last three weeks, Kaleb and Kaiyla went to their church building at 6:00 a.m. to meet with others to begin the day with an hour of prayer. Kaleb is the youth minister, so the majority of those meeting were young adults in middle-school and high-school. Additionally, Kaleb broadcasted the prayer sessions online through the periscope app, so even if people couldn't physically come to the building for prayer, they could join. We were very thankful for the online opportunity, since we live three hours away. We were also thankful for the encouragement to pray each morning.

It amazed me to see how many students awakened an hour earlier than normal to meet at the church to pray before school began. It also amazed me to see how much I looked forward to that hour each morning, setting our alarm clock an hour earlier than usual so we could prepare a cup of coffee and then join with the group to begin our day in prayer.

When Kaleb initially started the series, he explained how several students he ministered to had asked how to make prayer a part of their daily life, specifically when life is so busy. Teens are usually involved in school, a sports team (or two or three), another school activity (or two or three), and additional extracurricular activities as well. Adults are equally overwhelmed with time constraints due to jobs and children's activities.

One recommendation Kaleb made to improve prayer life really resonated because of the simplicity of the plan. He recommended we use the "First Fifteen" principle to begin living a prayer-filled life. The First Fifteen idea is this: begin each day devoting your first fifteen minutes to God, with five minutes in the Word, five minutes in Worship and five minutes in Prayer.

What a wonderful way to start each day, and what a great recommendation for today's youth…and adults. It's so easy to wake up already stressed about everything we need to accomplish before our head hits the pillow again. Taking fifteen minutes to let God steer your day is brilliant. Waking up a little earlier to give him an entire hour of prayer, like we've done for the past twenty-one days, is even better!

This Week: Do you have a prayer time set aside each day? If not, start with the First Fifteen. Then move on to try the 21 Days of Prayer. Send me an email at renee@reneeandrews.com, and if I know of a group currently participating in the 21 Days of Prayer, I will send you the link – it's always encouraging to know your joining others to begin the day in prayer!

My Prayer to Start this Week:

Those to Remember in Prayer this Week:

MONDAY, SEPTEMBER 12

"My command is this: Love each other as I have loved you."
John 15:12

One of my favorite quotes is by poet Maya Angelou: "I've learned that people will forget what you said, people will forget what you did, but people will never forget how you made them feel."

As I age, it seems I've forgotten more than I remember. I particularly have a difficult time with names from the past. For example, at my thirtieth high school reunion, I felt a moment of panic when I noticed no one wore nametags. I was counting on those nametags, and I found myself continually asking those around me about the identity of former classmates. It wasn't because they'd changed in appearance, but more because I simply couldn't place a name with a face.

However, there are some names from the past that are so crystal clear. Do you know which names those are? They are the names of people who made me feel special. The teacher in high school who cared enough about his students to ask about our spiritual lives, as well as our academic lives – Mr. Malcolm Edge. The woman who went out of her way to help me obtain a scholarship to college, even though she was a counselor at a different high school – Mrs. Frances Entrekin.

And as I realized that I remembered names of those who made me feel special because of how they treated me, I also realized that

I remember the names of those that I had the opportunity to serve. Specifically, twenty years ago, I spent a year working with the special needs class at Rene and Kaleb's elementary school. There were five children in the class, and I remember each and every one by name: Madeleine, MaryAnne, Ben, Sean and Mark.

Those five children in that special needs class didn't serve me in any capacity. They each had disabilities that hindered them from almost all forms of communication. However, they made me feel special, because they allowed me to do what Christ wants me to do, love others. God made us in His image, and God loves others. He loved us enough to send his Son to die for us. Therefore, it only makes sense that the way someone makes us feel isn't always equally yoked to what they have done for us. Often times, such as in the case of those wonderful children whose names are still written on my heart, the way someone makes us feel is more closely yoked to what God allowed us to do for the person...loving, the way Christ first loved us.

This Week: Locate your nearest special needs facility and ask if they have any current needs for volunteers. Offer one day a week, a month, or year. Enjoy the opportunity to serve and love the way Christ served and loved.

My Prayer to Start this Week:

Those to Remember in Prayer this Week:

MONDAY, SEPTEMBER 19

"I planted the seed, Apollos watered it, but God has been making it grow." ~ 1 Corinthians 3:6

I heard a story about a woman who, on her death bed, couldn't remember personally bringing a soul to Christ. She was dismayed that she had missed so many opportunities throughout her life on earth. Yet when she arrived at Heaven's gates, she saw a huge crowd gathered behind her, the souls to whom she had contributed something toward their salvation. Some were her children. Others were those she'd taught in Sunday school. And there were some she had met in brief acquaintance and never realized the impact she'd made on their lives.

In the verse above, Paul responded to an argument from disciples claiming to follow him or Apollos. He explained that though he and Apollos had a part, God made the seed grow. Yes, God is who we follow, rather than Paul or Apollos, but Paul's statement also reminds us that we can have a part, by planting a seed or watering it, nurturing the spirituality of others. And we should plant those seeds.

Recently I saw a photo of a man who attended high school with me over thirty years ago. He didn't graduate; he was in jail at the time of our graduation. In fact, the main thing I remember about him was that, though he was a very likeable guy, he always stood on the opposite side of the law and spent more years in alternative school than with the remainder of his class in public school. Every time I heard his name in passing, it was to inform me of the latest reason he'd ended up behind bars.

So the photo that I saw recently took me by surprise. He stood, smiling by a large cross in a church with a guitar at his side. It didn't take me long to find out that he's truly changed his life. He is part of a praise band, very involved in his church and on fire for his Lord.

After seeing the photo and learning about what had happened in his life, I immediately called my father and told him. I remembered that years ago, when my father was involved in a prison ministry, he'd started counseling with the young man in jail. Knowing I had graduated with him, Daddy asked me if I would write him a letter of encouragement, because he didn't get many visitors or correspondence, and Daddy thought it might lift his spirits. I wrote the letter. Daddy continued to minister to him in jail. And then, probably twenty-plus years later, we learn that his life has changed and that he's found Christ.

I thought Daddy would be so excited. I said, "Daddy, I'm sure you planted a seed when you ministered to him at the jail." And my father said, "You know, I'd forgotten all about that."

Daddy's comment reminded me of the story I heard about the woman who thought she hadn't brought anyone to Christ. And it reminded me that we may not even realize when we are planting seeds. I wonder how many other young men my father taught in the jail ministry eventually found their way to Christ. Won't it be awesome when Daddy finds out when he gets to Heaven? Won't it be awesome when we find out about seeds we never knew we planted?

This Week: Do one of the following to plant seeds at your local jail: 1) Donate Christian books – our local jail loves it when I donate some of my Christian fiction books for their inmates' library, 2) Start a card ministry where your church sends cards and notes of encouragement to those in jail, 3) Join or start a prison ministry and plant those seeds personally.

My Prayer to Start this Week:

Those to Remember in Prayer this Week:

MONDAY, SEPTEMBER 26

"But about that day or hour no one knows, not even the angels in heaven, nor the Son, but only the Father." ~ Mark 13:32

On the day I am writing this devotion, the world is supposed to end.

<insert shaking of my head, followed by a loud sigh>

I am writing this on September 27, 2015, which, according to some Biblical scholars, will be the last day of the world's existence. Tonight, a rare blood moon (or supermoon) will occur when the moon is at the closest point of its elliptical orbit around Earth, which is called perigee. I am planning to join many others tonight to attempt to see the event (where I live, the best time to watch will be between 9:00 p.m. and 10:00 p.m.); however, I do not expect to see Christ appear following the occurrence, as many are predicting.

Throughout my life, I can recall several times when someone has predicted the end of time and Christ's return. The fact that many of these people are preachers or Biblical scholars surprises me the most. Haven't they read the verses in the Bible where we learn that not even Christ knows the day of His return? So the fact that so many are expecting His return today verifies that this day isn't the one.

When I was in elementary school, several of my classmates had heard the world would end on a certain date (1975). At that point, I was too young and naïve to be certain they weren't telling the truth, and I was a bit nervous. I also remember Daddy reassuring that no one knew the day or hour when Christ would come. The next "big date" that I remember was Y2K. So many thought the world would end on January 1, 2000 that they were behaving as such on December 31, 1999. We lived in Atlanta at the time and remained at home that night rather than going anywhere to celebrate the New Year. Why? Because so many believed that would be the last night of the world as they knew it, and they were quite honestly trying to go out with a bang.

Nowadays, whenever something like today's supermoon event occurs, I find comfort, not so much because I am certain no one will predict the actual day of Christ's return, but in the fact that if He comes today, tomorrow, or whenever, I am ready. Ready to see my loved ones who've passed on. Ready to go to Heaven with my family and friends at my side. And most certainly ready to finally, blessedly be with my Savior. Come quickly, Lord!

This Week: If you have access to a computer, search for "end of time predictions." I found 242 in my search today. By the time this book is published and you perform your search, there will undoubtedly be more. See if you can remember when you heard about any of those predictions. Take comfort in the fact that those days have come and gone. But take more comfort in the fact that the true date will come, and that you are ready to meet your Lord!

My Prayer to Start this Week:

Those to Remember in Prayer this Week:

MONDAY, OCTOBER 3

"Therefore, since we are surrounded by such a great cloud of witnesses, let us throw off everything that hinders and the sin that so easily entangles. And let us run with perseverance the race marked out for us, fixing our eyes on Jesus, the pioneer and perfecter of faith. For the joy set before him he endured the cross, scorning its shame, and sat down at the right hand of the throne of God." ~ Hebrews 12:1-2

When our oldest son was in high school, he played football and was quite talented at interceptions. In fact, during his senior year, he had the most interceptions in the state. As a parent, it's a lot of fun to watch your child snag a pass intended for someone else, and even more fun when he takes it all the way to the end zone, which Rene did on several occasions that year.

Now I can tell you with complete honesty that my mother, or MiMi, is the type of grandmother who never misses a grandchild's activity (my father, aka PopPop, is the same way). MiMi is known for her excitement at her grandkids' games. She cheers. She dances. She encourages them from the stands (loud enough that all of the players know her by sight *and* by voice). And on one night, she was headed to the concession stand for a snack when Rene snagged an interception and took off down the field.

Rene said he could hear her, as always, but she seemed much closer than usual. And as he sprinted down the field, he saw why. My mother, his grandmother, was running along the fence beside him, cheering the whole way. "Go, Rene! You can do it, Rene! Go, go, go!" She ran the distance to the end zone and then jumped up and down as though she were one of the high school cheerleaders on the sideline.

He loved it and still tells the story often. I think part of it was because it was his MiMi, and no other player has a grandmother quite like her. But I think another part of it was that he wasn't running the distance along and was cheered on throughout the journey by someone who knew he could reach his goal.

One of my favorite contemporary Christian songs is *Cloud of Witnesses* by Mark Schultz. I'd never really thought of a cloud of witnesses surrounding us, such as described in Hebrews 12, until I heard that song. The imagery he portrays, of fellow Christians throughout our life rooting us on and lifting us up through our journey toward the goal, is beautiful. And I think of all of the people in my life who, like my mom at that football game, are running beside me in my spiritual journey, knowing we will reach that end zone and claim the prize of eternity with Christ.

This Week: If you have access to a computer, search for the song Cloud of Witnesses by Mark Schultz. Listen to the lyrics. Thank someone who is cheering you on, and cheer others on throughout your journey. How exciting it will be when you reach that finish line and celebrate together with your Lord!

My Prayer to Start this Week:

Those to Remember in Prayer this Week:

MONDAY, OCTOBER 10

"Jesus rebuked the demon, and it came out of the boy, and he was healed at that moment. Then the disciples came to Jesus in private and asked, "Why couldn't we drive it out?" He replied, "Because you have so little faith. Truly I tell you, if you have faith as small as a mustard seed, you can say to this mountain, 'Move from here to there,' and it will move. Nothing will be impossible for you." ~ *Matthew 17:18-20*

J.R.'s business car is a Smart ForTwo. We drive it often, partly because it is wrapped in the gym logo and is a great advertisement, and also because it gets an average of fifty miles per gallon. However, we rarely use the car without having at least one person ask, "Do you feel safe in that little thing?"

In truth, the Smart car, designed by Mercedes, has a steel cage surrounding the occupants that is similar to the type that protects racecar drivers. And it has eight airbags. Plus, if you watch the abundance of videos regarding the safety of the car and the tests taken to ensure its protection abilities, you will agree with me when I joke that, "It's a steel cage with eight airbags; we would be more likely to suffocate from the bags than be injured." And no, I don't think we would actually suffocate. But my point is this: even though that car is tiny (it has been on a sidewalk before, as you may have read in one of my other devotions), it's unbelievably safe and strong. One commercial shows the steel cage of a Smart ForTwo beneath a full-sized SUV and holding its own just fine.

A mustard seed averages one to two millimeters. Tiny. Yet Christ used that teeny seed to illustrate the power of faith. I'm not sure what you do when you can feel your faith wavering in a situation, but whenever I feel myself starting to doubt whether something could be possible (maybe I'm uttering a prayer and, at the same time, wondering whether it could occur), I silently tell myself to, "Stay above the water."

What does that mean? It means I think about Peter, walking on the water toward Christ, and even though he had the ability to see his Lord and Savior ahead, his faith still faltered, and he began to sink. If he'd have had faith the size of a mustard seed, based on what Christ has said, he would have remained above the waves.

It's sometimes much easier to doubt than to believe; however, we have been assured that if we can hang on to that faith, even in the smallest doses, we will remain safe. We will stay above the water.

This Week: When your faith tries to dwindle, think about my tiny car or that teeny mustard seed Christ used in His parable. Remember what even a small amount of faith can accomplish and remind yourself to stay above the water.

My Prayer to Start this Week:

Those to Remember in Prayer this Week:

MONDAY, OCTOBER 17

"Remember the former things, those of long ago; I am God, and there is no other; I am God, and there is none like me. I make known the end from the beginning, from ancient times, what is still to come. I say, 'My purpose will stand, and I will do all that I please." ~ Isaiah 46:9-10

I love being a grandmother, or a "KK," as the grandkids call me. There is an indescribable joy to being able to take care of children without being the primary disciplinarian. Honestly, in my eyes, they do no wrong (but that's the way grandparents see things, isn't it?).

However, as I'm often reminded by our son, when he's describing the latest shenanigans the grandboys have been into (and I'm trying not to laugh), children are far from perfect. Recently, Rene shared this insight on Facebook:

The boys are now getting in a phase that can be tough; they are starting to think that they know some stuff, how things should work, etc. Occasionally, they disagree with us, voicing that disagreement and even "talking back." They are quickly learning that they shouldn't continue this behavior, but whenever it happens, I want to turn and say, "I am twenty-six years old. Your mom is twenty-four. You are seven. Seven! We have finished school, graduated college, been successful in the work place for years. You know nothing. You have done nothing. Who do you think you are?"

And then, Rene concluded his post with this:

NOW: My point here is this: God continues to use these boys to give me a little picture of what it is like for Him to deal with me.

Didn't he nail it? We all think we know so much, but we know nothing. God knows all. I have to think that each time I question why something has happened, the "Why do bad things happen to good people?" mentality, God's response would be similar to Rene's response to the boys, or to God's own response to Job in Job 38: "Where were you when I laid the earth's foundation?"

This Week: Are you tempted to question something in your life now? Do you know someone suffering through a hardship or a disease, or are you the one suffering? Pray for peace and for the ability to remember that we know nothing, God knows all, and regardless of the pain on this earth, the best is truly yet to come.

My Prayer to Start this Week:

Those to Remember in Prayer this Week:

MONDAY, OCTOBER 24

"The generous will themselves be blessed, for they share their food with the poor." ~ Proverbs 22:9

A few weeks ago, we drove to Atlanta with Rene, Ariel, Alanus and Jerry to shop for furniture at IKEA. Our first granddaughter, Naomi, is due in December, and we are helping Rene and Ariel get their house ready for the precious new arrival.

As we neared the traffic light before the large store, we saw a homeless man standing at the edge of the road holding a sign saying he was hungry and needed help. None of us had cash to give the man, but Rene had brought along a grocery bag filled with scuppernongs, Rene's favorite fruit. In fact, Rene says his two favorite seasons are Christmas and scuppernong-season, the time in the fall when the fruit is ripe and ready to eat.

In case you aren't familiar, a scuppernong is yellowish-green, larger than a grape but smaller than a plum, and absolutely delicious. Yes, they have seeds, but the taste is so amazing that you won't care.

So on the day we went shopping, Rene saw the homeless man and, realizing we didn't have anything to offer him, remembered the bag of his favorite treats. He rolled the window down and asked the man if he would like a bag of scuppernongs. His face was wrinkled and covered in a beard, but his eyes lit up when he saw the bag of fruit. "Really?" he asked. Rene nodded and handed over the bag. And while we sat at the red light, the man pulled out a scuppernong and ate it, then shook his head and said, "These take me back to my youth, son. Thank you."

I still get choked up simply remembering how it felt to see something as simple as a bag of fruit provide a man who has had tough times a cherished memory. Isn't it amazing, how God gives us exactly what we need to help others, even when we don't realize the tools in our care. And sometimes, what we need is as small and simple as a bag of fruit, but even with something that seems so small, God shows how He is so very big.

This Week: Host a care bag night. Ask members or your Bible study group or church class to bring small items that could be used by the homeless and will fit in gallon bags to your next gathering. Work together to assemble these care bags and then distribute them through the group, so that the next time you see a homeless man or woman, you will have something useful to offer. Ideas for bag items: granola bars or other similar pre-packaged food items, a toothbrush, toothpaste, soap, shampoo, lotion, socks.

My Prayer to Start this Week:

Those to Remember in Prayer this Week:

MONDAY, OCTOBER 31

"Some went out on the sea in ships; they were merchants on the mighty waters. They saw the works of the Lord, his wonderful deeds in the deep. For he spoke and stirred up a tempest that lifted high the waves. They mounted up to the heavens and went down to the depths; in their peril their courage melted away. They reeled and staggered like drunkards; they were at their wits' end. Then they cried out to the Lord in their trouble, and he brought them out of their distress. He stilled the storm to a whisper; the waves of the sea were hushed. They were glad when it grew calm, and he guided them to their desired haven. Let them give thanks to the Lord for his unfailing love and his wonderful deeds for mankind."
~ Psalm 107:23-31

Many understand the dangers of tornados. We've all seen the results on news broadcasts or even firsthand. Fewer people are familiar with the dangers of straight-line winds, but I've experienced a storm of straight-line winds that I honestly thought would demolish our house. We had two huge trees in our front yard. Both were uprooted. One fell into the house, plowing through the roof and allowing rain to dump into our living room, while I watched from the kitchen. You may wonder why I hadn't sought better shelter; it was because I didn't have time. Straight-line winds often give little to no warning, and I didn't realize what was happening until the windows started to rattle and the trees flipped over.

So when my husband called me from Mississippi a few months

later and told me he thought he was traveling through another straight-line windstorm, I immediately pulled up the weather radar on my computer to see exactly what was happening on that portion of the interstate. I'm very thankful his cell phone produced a signal; he couldn't get any signal on the radio and wasn't sure what was happening around him. Sure enough, he was heading directly into another unexpected straight-line storm. With him still on the line, I located another route and talked him through the detour to keep him out of the main brunt of the winds and to a safe location.

The situation reminded me of how often we're hit with unexpected trials in life. Like those windstorms, things often happen that we can't see coming and aren't prepared to handle. However, as referenced in the verses above, God provides everything we need to make it through the storm. And, in the same manner that I guided J.R. away from the danger, He provides His Word to guide us through life's struggles. We simply need to remember that we have everything we need, and there is no shame in asking for help from the One who has always been able to calm the storm.

This Week: You undoubtedly have at least one major struggle or worry in your world right now. Stop trying to navigate your way on your own, and call on the One who can guide you safely through the storm. Feel the peace of knowing He can set your toppled world right again.

My Prayer to Start this Week:

Those to Remember in Prayer this Week:

MONDAY, NOVEMBER 7

"Brothers and sisters, if someone is caught in a sin, you who live by the Spirit should restore that person gently. But watch yourselves, or you also may be tempted. Carry each other's burdens, and in this way you will fulfill the law of Christ."
Galatians 6:1-2

At the time that I'm writing this devotional, our youngest son, Kaleb, and our sweet daughter-in-law, Kaiyla, are hiking through a state park in Colorado. They left Alabama four days ago. We heard from them when they arrived in Denver two days ago, and we haven't heard from them since.

Now, after we tried to call yesterday and found that their phones are either out of power or turned off, we realized several errors on our part (and theirs too, I suppose): 1) we had no idea where they were hiking in Colorado, 2) we didn't remind them to conserve the batteries on their phones in case they had an emergency, 3) we weren't certain whether they would be in the woods for five days straight, or whether they would come out, say, to catch a phone signal and let us know they were breathing.

As you can imagine, I've been doing a lot of one-on-one conversing with my Heavenly Father over the past few days, asking Him to keep them safe, begging Him to let us hear from them, and letting Him know how very much we love them and want to know that they are both okay.

And as J.R. and I comprehend how we need to verify the

physical safety of our kids, I also am reminded how we also need to regularly verify their spiritual safety too. In fact, our daily morning prayers will vary somewhat, but we always pray for our family to be good examples and lead others to Christ. However, I know that Christ doesn't merely expect us to be accountability partners with the members of our family; we should do the same for our fellow brothers and sisters in Christ, as the verse indicates above. We are to bear each other's burdens and restore one another gently.

Is it tough to ask our twenty-four year old son and his twenty-two year old wife to check in? Does it feel like we're invading their space? Maybe a little. But thankfully, they both understand that we want/need to make certain they are safe.

Is it tough to ask our fellow Christians to check in, particularly if we know they are vulnerable and facing a difficult temptation? Does it feel like we're invading their space? Maybe. But if we do it gently, as the verse indicates, they will hopefully understand that we want/need to make certain their souls are safe.

This Week: When you're checking on the physical safety of your family and friends, remember to check on their spiritual safety too. I pray that you receive a heartfelt, "Thanks," for checking in and gratitude that you care...like the message I just received from Kaiyla letting me know that they are in Rocky Mountain National Park, and they're fine! Praise God!

My Prayer to Start this Week:

Those to Remember in Prayer this Week:

MONDAY, NOVEMBER 14

"Above all, love each other deeply, because love covers over a multitude of sins. Offer hospitality to one another without grumbling. Each of you should use whatever gift you have received to serve others, as faithful stewards of God's grace in its various forms. If anyone speaks, they should do so as one who speaks the very words of God. If anyone serves, they should do so with the strength God provides, so that in all things God may be praised through Jesus Christ. To him be the glory and the power for ever and ever. Amen." ~ 1 Peter 4:8-11

We have a nineteen-year old young lady from our church currently serving in missions for two years in Honduras. At nineteen, I was in college and couldn't fathom giving two years of my life to God. In fact, that was probably one of the weakest times for faith in my entire life. Yet this young girl, Tristen, made the commitment with a smile.

When Tristen announced her decision earlier this year, my heart swelled with admiration. She's a beautiful young girl with the world ahead of her…and she chose to go to another country and teach others about Christ.

That was roughly six months ago, and last Sunday our church announced that Tristen had asked for prayers and that she was starting to feel homesick. We all prayed for Tristen, and then our life group (small Bible study group) decided to send a care package to encourage Tristen through the difficult times away from her family and friends. We asked her mom for a list of things she might like, and this is the list we received: cards of encouragement, Velveeta macaroni, Nutella, beef jerky, Dr. Pepper, long-sleeved t-shirts, razors, lotions and dry shampoo.

I sent the list to our group, and within one day, we had an abundance of every item. Our youth group at church, Tristen's peers, were thrilled to write notes of encouragement for us to include with our care package, and each life group member was grateful for the opportunity to serve our young sister in Christ.

The Bible has numerous scriptures about encouraging each other, but often, we get so wrapped up in the business of our own lives that we neglect an opportunity to uplift one another. Tristen's list was simple, yet I didn't think to ask what we could do to encourage her until the church announced she needed prayers.

In the future, I want to do my best to keep my eyes open for opportunities to encourage others. I'm going to pray for God to show me what I can do to help, to encourage, to love the way Christ loved us. That's what it's all about, right? (John 13:35)

This Week: Send a card of encouragement or a care package to a young missionary. Email me at renee@reneeandrews.com if you'd like help finding a name and address.

My Prayer to Start this Week:

Those to Remember in Prayer this Week:

MONDAY, NOVEMBER 21

"Be very careful, then, how you live—not as unwise but as wise, making the most of every opportunity, because the days are evil. Therefore, do not be foolish, but understand what the Lord's will is." ~ Ephesians 5:15-17

My laptop died. Again. This is the second computer that has nearly given me heart failure when I turn the thing on and nothing happens. Both times, thanks to a computer-savvy husband and a terrific Internet service provider, all of my files have been recovered, which is great, because both times, I had procrastinated performing a backup.

When we learned that the latest laptop was no longer functional, J.R. surprised me with a new MacBook. I've never used a Mac, and like most people, I'm not a fan of change, but I'm attempting to learn. So, in the process of reorganizing all of the files on my backup, I saw names of books long forgotten, things I've written over the past decade that I never finished. I have sketches of ideas that were never developed. I have some books with over two hundred pages written that I never finished.

In my case, the reason for abandoning a project typically means I had been paid to finish something else. When I sign a book contract, I'm paid an advance for my work, and therefore, that project moves up in my priority above a new proposal, something that hasn't been pitched to my agent or editor. Still, I always plan to return to the work in progress and complete the task. However, in almost every case, I didn't. As a result, I have an abundance of unfinished manuscripts in a mass of files on my new computer.

I want to finish the books. I want to write "The End" on every one. And I'm fairly certain that I've had the opportunity to do so throughout the years that I left them hanging on my hard drive.

I'm reminded of Paul, in Romans 7:15, when he said, "I do not understand what I do. For what I want to do I do not do, but what I hate I do." Paul referred to our sinful nature, but his comment could also apply to our procrastinating nature. We put things off, leave things undone. Sometimes, as in the case of my books, no harm is done by our actions (except, in my case, I have some readers who truly want to know the next segment to a certain story). But if the thing we are putting off is Christ, much damage is done by our actions. Or should I say lack of action?

What if we put off a conversation with a loved one, that conversation that is oh-so-difficult but oh-so-life-changing, the one where we tell them they need Christ? What if we put off prioritizing Christ in our own life? That kind of procrastination produces much more than unhappy readers; that kind of procrastination can cost souls.

This Week: Is there someone in your life that you've meant to tell about Christ but haven't found the time or courage? Find an opportunity to make that call, have that conversation or invite him/her to church. Feel the joy of overcoming procrastination; moreover, feel the joy of saving a soul!

My Prayer to Start this Week:

Those to Remember in Prayer this Week:

MONDAY, NOVEMBER 28

"Jesus said to his disciples: "Things that cause people to stumble are bound to come, but woe to anyone through whom they come. It would be better for them to be thrown into the sea with a millstone tied around their neck than to cause one of these little ones to stumble. So watch yourselves. If your brother or sister sins against you, rebuke them; and if they repent, forgive them" ~ Luke 17:1-3

Time heals all things. I've heard that saying as long as I can remember, and at one time, I'd have probably said that it was true; however, when it comes to offenses, I'd say time magnifies the pain.

Over the years, I've learned that the longer we harbor feelings of hurt or resentment, the stronger they become. We replay the act over and over, intensifying the transgression with each memory. And this reaction is exactly what we aren't supposed to do.

Time *doesn't* heal all things; Christ does. We need Him to resolve those differences, and He has given us the tools we need for healing our pain. We are to forgive as He forgives. If our brother or sister sins against us, we are to rebuke them; if they repent, we are to forgive.

I've had friends who, when discussing how they had been hurt by someone, downplayed the issue. For example, they might dismiss the action with, "Oh, it wasn't that bad," or "She didn't mean it in that way." But I've learned that minimizing the offense minimizes the forgiveness. Trust me, I know. Christ gave us examples of forgiveness because He knows how important it is to forgive, as well as that true healing can't come by ignoring a problem and allowing it to mushroom into something beyond its original form.

If you've been hurt, let the person know. Assuming they know how you feel isn't the answer; tell them how you feel and why. Then forgiveness can occur. How can someone repent if they are unaware of the transgression? We've all been hurt at one time or another. We've all hurt someone, whether intentionally or unintentionally, at one time or another. But Christ gave us the perfect example, His death on the cross, to show us that we have every capability to forgive. And true forgiveness is a beautiful thing. Cleansing. Healing. He showed us how. We simply need to follow His lead.

This Week: Have you been harboring a pain toward an individual? Does your heart ache when you recall the closeness you once shared and the distance that divides you now? Take the first step. Reach out and let that person know. And if you're the one who needs to forgive a wrongdoing, ask God to help you as you turn the pain over to Him and give that person what they need—forgiveness.

My Prayer to Start this Week:

Those to Remember in Prayer this Week:

MONDAY, DECEMBER 5

"The eyes of the Lord are on the righteous, and his ears are attentive to their cry; but the face of the Lord is against those who do evil, to blot out their name from the earth. The righteous cry out, and the Lord hears them; he delivers them from all their troubles. The Lord is close to the brokenhearted and saves those who are crushed in spirit." ~ Psalm 34:15-18

Sometimes I need to remind myself that God's promise to deliver us from all of our troubles may not have anything to do with ridding us of our earthly struggles. In fact, I'm certain that it doesn't, or why would any of us suffer?

Today I learned of a young man who had graduated high school and started his first college semester. The world awaited his arrival. He had a large, loving Christian family. They're the type of group that appear as though nothing could keep them from smiling. Faithful. Giving to others. Following Christ's example.

And yet today, they lost their son in a tragic auto accident. He'd started school away from home and was doing well, thriving, making new friends and establishing the groundwork for a full and successful life. But that life was cut short. And the cheerful family from yesterday is mourning today.

I have prayed for his family, for the friends he'd recently left when he moved away and for the friends he'd made in his new life. But I have also prayed to thank God that he has a brand new life today, because our Heavenly Father also had a Son who suffered, so that when we suffer, even to the extent that the family is suffering today, we can be assured that God will deliver us from the pain. He will deliver us from the troubles of this world. We will find peace again, regardless of our circumstances here, when we arrive at our heavenly home, the way that son found peace when he went home today, and the way his family will find peace when they are reunited with him again.

This Week: Purchase a box of sympathy cards. Be sure to let those who have lost loved ones this year know that you are thinking of them as they enter their first holiday season without their loved ones.

My Prayer to Start this Week:

Those to Remember in Prayer this Week:

MONDAY, DECEMBER 12

"So when you give to the needy, do not announce it with trumpets, as the hypocrites do in the synagogues and on the streets, to be honored by others. Truly I tell you, they have received their reward in full. But when you give to the needy, do not let your left hand know what your right hand is doing, so that your giving may be in secret. Then your Father, who sees what is done in secret, will reward you." ~ Matthew 6:2-4

Does everyone have a grandparent who scared them a little when they were young? My Paw-Paw Bowers had that effect on me and, I assume, on all twelve of his grandchildren. He was tall, around six-foot-three, intimidating for any child, but he also had a gruffness to him that kept the grandchildren in line when Granny spoiled us rotten. And at times when he was overly happy, one of his favorite things to do was yell, "Eskiboodie!" as he popped his false teeth out of his mouth at you and then whisked them back inside…while the grandkids squealed. To this day, I have no idea what "Eskiboodie" means; it was simply his word when he teased us.

But in spite of the intimidation I often felt around Paw-Paw, I would occasionally spot glimpses of the soft heart behind the tough exterior. And those glimpses, some I'm certain he has no idea I would remember, have held true when other memories of the past have long faded, because of the impression they left on my soul.

I remember one Christmas when a man who worked as a hired

hand on Paw-Paw's farm was having a difficult time providing for his family, not because Paw-Paw didn't pay him well, but because he was addicted to alcohol and spent his earnings on liquor. I saw the abundance of packages in Paw-Paw's truck, and then I saw them again the next morning on the family's front porch. He made certain that family enjoyed Christmas, but he never mentioned his actions.

And I remember how several of Paw-Paw's neighbors enjoyed the fruits of his labor in his garden. We always had fresh turnip greens, tomatoes, corn, beans, okra and peas. Paw-Paw would take grocery sacks of vegetables and leave them on the porches of the people who lived in "The Bend," the beautiful neighborhood that I still call "home."

Looking back, I'm certain there were more times he generously gave without desiring or wanting acknowledgement. He may have had a gruff exterior, but his heart knew the beauty of giving, and even though I only saw glimpses, his actions had a tremendous effect on his second-oldest-granddaughter. I wanted to be like Paw-Paw. I wanted to be like Christ.

This Week: If you have the means and opportunity, at a fast food drive-through (my favorite is Chic-fil-A), pay for the next car's meal.

My Prayer to Start this Week:

Those to Remember in Prayer this Week:

MONDAY, DECEMBER 19

"You alone are the Lord. You made the heavens, even the highest heavens, and all their starry host, the earth and all that is on it, the seas and all that is in them. You give life to everything, and the multitudes of heaven worship you." ~ Nehemiah 9:6

On a recent walk, I saw one of our elderly neighbors working in his garage. He looked very involved in his work, so it surprised me when he glanced up, waved and asked if I'd like to take a look at his current woodworking project.

Entering the garage, I was amazed. Wooden creations lined the walls, and on this particular day, he was building shelves that would display his collection of miniature motorcycles. Until then, I didn't realize he enjoyed working with wood, but it was obvious by the smile on his face when he showed me his work that he truly loves the beauty of creating.

As I left from our visit, I thought about the natural desire God gave us to enjoy creating. I see it at such an early age through my grandchildren, building something out of Legos or coloring a picture for my refrigerator. I think about my sister, an artist, and the fulfillment she receives when she takes a few tubes of paint and creates a beautiful piece for galleries. And I feel it myself when I put words together to form a story, or a devotional that can be used to glorify God.

God created us in His image. And He is the ultimate Creator. Is it any wonder that we enjoy experiencing a semblance of what He did in the beginning? And can we even fathom the joy He had when He created His perfect masterpiece? How blessed we are to have been formed by the One who not only created all, and what a blessing that He placed the joy of creating in each of us!

This Week: Create something—it doesn't have to be anything elaborate—draw a picture, help your children or grandchildren build a fort with sheets, write a poem. Let yourself be reminded of the joy of creating while you praise God for His masterpiece.

My Prayer to Start this Week:

Those to Remember in Prayer this Week:

MONDAY, DECEMBER 26

"While they were there, the time came for the baby to be born, and she gave birth to her firstborn, a son. She wrapped him in cloths and placed him in a manger, because there was no guest room available for them." Luke 2:6-7

As I write this devotion, our family is planning for the birth of our fifth grandchild, our first granddaughter. She should arrive shortly before Christmas, and we are thrilled about the beauty of having a new baby to celebrate during the holiday season. Many preparations have been made, since the day in March when Rene and Ariel told us they were expecting a baby.

One of the things that immediately came to mind for them in their planning was that they believed they needed more room for their newest addition. They already have our two oldest grandsons, and there wasn't an additional bedroom in the house for the little girl that would arrive soon. So they started looking at homes with a little more space, and then they started meeting with contractors about the possibility of adding on. Finally, they selected a contractor and started going through the endless steps of getting a loan for the construction.

This week, they got down to the final day before closing the loan and knew construction would finally begin (the baby is due in thirteen weeks), but the night before they were set to close, the contractor backed out of the job. With time running out and no additional contractor proposals on the table, Rene and Ariel took another look at their situation and decided God might be leading them to make things work with the space they already have. Thus, we have spent the past few days rearranging their home and determining how to make it work. And it will. Everything is going to be just fine, and they will have the perfect space for Naomi when she arrives.

In watching them go through the disappointments and changing plans, I thought about the verse above, when Joseph and Mary went to Bethlehem and found "no room in the inn." Now, obviously God knew they were going to Bethlehem. He'd planned this blessed event and foreshadowed it throughout time perfectly. Everything built up to this moment when our Lord and Savior would enter the world and obtain victory over sin. All of the details were in place to fulfill every prophecy. Nothing was left to chance. God even inspired the census that took them to Bethlehem.

Yet there was no room in the inn.

Now, do you think our omniscient, omnipresent and omnipotent Creator forgot that detail? Of course not. He could have had an entire inn, an entire city, waiting with empty rooms. Why didn't He have an open room at the inn? Naturally, I do not know the answer to that question, but with our recent situation with Rene and Ariel, I have started to wonder if God wasn't revealing insight to His perfect plan. Even with something as monumental as the birth of His Son, God showed us that just because things don't fall perfectly into place, that doesn't mean He isn't in control or that He has let us down. God's perfect plan can sometimes be messy, and as we grow in our walk with Him, it might get even messier. But how much greater can our faith be when we know that, even when we encounter the pitfalls of life, those pitfalls were put there by a great and mighty, ever-loving, ever-caring and ever-present Father!

This Week: Are you planning a big event, perhaps the arrival of a new child or grandchild? Have you thought of every detail that will make everything absolutely perfect? If you have, that's great, but remember that when things fall apart, everything seems to unravel and you feel control of your world slipping...the world isn't yours to control. Hand it over to the One who actually controls our world, the messy parts and all, and let Him show you that even something that doesn't seem perfect...may very well be His perfect plan all along!

My Prayer to Start this Week:

Those to Remember in Prayer this Week:

AUTHOR BIO:

National Readers' Choice Award winner and RT Reviewers' Choice Award winner Renee Andrews spends a lot of time in the gym. No, she isn't working out. Her husband, a former All-American gymnast, owns a cheerleading and tumbling gym. She is thankful the talented kids at the gym don't have a problem when she brings her laptop and writes while they sweat. When she isn't writing, she's typically traveling with her husband, bragging about their sons and daughters-in-law or spoiling their grandchildren.

Renee is a kidney donor and actively supports organ donation. In 2013, Renee, her husband J.R. and their oldest son Rene competed as team Hello Kidney on the American Bible Challenge to raise money for living donors and to raise awareness for the need for living donors. If you are considering becoming a living donor, ask her about how you can also save a life by sharing your spare. Or check out the "living donor" section of her website.

She welcomes prayer requests and loves to hear from readers. Write her at Renee@ReneeAndrews.com or visit her at her website.

Renee Andrews on Facebook:
www.facebook.com/AuthorReneeAndrews
Renee Andrews on Twitter:
www.twitter.com/reneeandrews
To purchase autographed copies of Renee's devotionals, visit
www.MondayswithJesus.com

www.ingramcontent.com/pod-product-compliance
Lightning Source LLC
Chambersburg PA
CBHW031535040426
42445CB00010B/552